I0796466

THE POETRY OF
Chūya Nakahara

JAPAN'S MODERNIST MASTER

translated and introduced by
Christian Nagle

foreword by
Mikirō Sasaki

TUTTLE Publishing
Tokyo | Rutland, Vermont | Singapore

Contents

SONGS OF BYGONE DAYS

Foreword

by Mikirō Sasaki

Chūya Nakahara's *Goat Songs* and *Songs of Bygone Days*

Chūya Nakahara (1907–1937) is a crucial figure in the emergence of modern Japanese poetry, which laid the foundations for contemporary Japanese verse.

During his short thirty-year life, he left behind two poetry collections, *Goat Songs* (1934) and *Songs of Bygone Days* (1938). In addition to his own poetry, he translated numerous works by poets of the French Symbolist movement and published several volumes of Arthur Rimbaud's poetry in Japanese translation. His original works, as well as his translations, had a profound impact on later generations of Japanese poets.

With the publication of this English translation of Chūya's *Goat Songs* and *Songs of Bygone Days*, I am delighted to help introduce to English-language readers a poet who devoted his entire being to poetry, relentlessly exploring what poetry is and what it means to be a poet.

Chūya lived as though poetry and life were inseparable. One could say he engaged with poetry with his whole body and mind. Since his time, there has been no other poet like him in Japan.

He began writing poetry seriously at sixteen, and when he died at thirty, he had spent a mere fifteen years in poetic creation. However, this span—from the late Taishō era to the early years of Shōwa—coincided with an era of linguistic upheaval.

First, this was the final stage in the transition from classical literary language to the modern colloquial style.

Second, around this time, original texts of contemporary

European poetry were reaching Japan at an unprecedented rate, thanks to the completion of the Trans-Siberian Railway, which enabled books to arrive in as little as two weeks. Western literary magazines and books also became more affordable. This meant that young poets like Chūya were in a position to personally select, absorb and translate European poetry. Until then, Western poetry had been introduced into Japan primarily by scholars and those with experience studying abroad.

Third, from the mid-Taishō period onward, traditional Japanese fixed forms (tanka and haiku) and free verse established distinct domains. Free verse, imported from the West in the Meiji era, began to affirm its raison d'être in Japan. Henceforth, Japanese poetry diverged into three competing genres: tanka, with its fixed rhythm of 5-7-5-7-7 morae (syllables that, in Japanese, also count double consonants, long vowels, and word-closing "n"s); haiku, with its 5-7-5 pattern; and free verse, which had no prescribed rhythmic structure.

These forces shaped Chūya as a poet. Unconsciously, he responded to the demands of his time. Of course, had he not been attuned to the fundamental issues within poetic language, he could have ignored them entirely. There was no obligation for him to shoulder the entire burden of Japanese poetic diction alone—he could have simply pursued the areas that interested him. Yet, in hindsight, if there is such a thing as a higher path in poetry, Chūya deliberately sought it out and walked it.

The Meaning Behind *Goat Songs*

Chūya's first poetry collection, *Goat Songs* (*Yagi no Uta*), comprises five sections: Early Poems, Boyhood, Michiko, Autumn and Sheep Songs. While Sheep Songs appears as a section title, the word "goat" does not actually appear in any of the poems. Why, then, did Chūya name his collection *Goat Songs*?

Several explanations are possible. According to a friend of Chūya's, the poet would often say that his own thin face and prominent ears made him resemble a goat. He also, upon seeing a photograph of Stéphane Mallarmé, felt a certain kinship with the French poet, whose sharp facial features reminded him of his own.

Chūya was born in the city of Yamaguchi, where his father was a well-known doctor and the director of Nakahara Clinic. To provide nourishment for his patients, the hospital kept goats and gave patients goat's milk. As a boy, Chūya often took them to the fields to play.

Additionally, in the Book of Leviticus in the Old Testament, the goat is described as a sacrificial offering for atonement. In Christian tradition, goats have been associated with sacrificial rites. Moreover, the Greek word for "tragedy," τραγωδία (*tragōidia*), literally means "goat song." In ancient Greek theater, the chorus was said to have worn goat masks while performing.

It is unclear whether Chūya deliberately traced the etymology of "tragedy" before choosing the title for his first poetry collection, but given that his adoptive grandparents were devout Christians and that he was exposed to the Bible from an early age, he must have known that goats were considered sacrificial animals.

The first section of the final poem in *Goat Songs*, "Voice of Life," contains the following lines:

> Sometimes I ask, as though kidding myself,
> Is it a woman? Something sweet? Or is it honor?
> Then my heart screams, It isn't that! It isn't this! It's neither that nor this!
> Then is it a song of the sky—a sky song that echoes, mornings, through the stratosphere?

In the next section, the poem continues:

> No matter what, it cannot be described!

Here, Chūya interrogates the nature of his own poetic longing and, in the process of answering that he cannot explain it, questions the meaning of existence. The final stanza of "Voice of Life" is as follows:

> Evening, under the sky, feeling the singularity of self, one has no complaints about anything.

This is the portrait of a man who knew no other way to live but through poetry. There are many ways to get by in the world. But what does it mean to choose to write poetry? At his most extreme, Chūya went so far as to write these lines, from the poem "Sheep Song":

> May I die face up!
> May not this small chin become smaller still!
> Yes, I am blamed for what I have
> not felt—an invocation to death, I believe.

Death is the punishment for failing to feel everything life has to offer. Longing for the absolute liberation of the senses, he appeared in the world as though he were a scapegoat for humanity itself.

The Evolution of "Song" in Chūya's Poetry

Both of Chūya's collections, *Goat Songs* and *Songs of Bygone Days*, contain the word "song" (*uta*, 歌) in their titles. Consider this line from "Voice of Life":

> Then is it a song of the sky—a sky song that echoes, mornings, through the stratosphere?

What did "song" mean to Chūya?

Tracing this concept through his work, one finds that the idea of "song" becomes increasingly clear as he moves from his first collection to his second. *Songs of Bygone Days* contains one of his representative works, "Cloudy Sky":

> One morning, up in the sky,
> I saw a fluttering black flag.
> It fluttered in the wind,
> but so high I couldn't hear the sound.
>
> I tried to reel it down, but since
> that couldn't happen without a rope,
> the flag continued to flutter,
> dancing into the depths of the sky.
>
> I think of how often I saw the like
> on mornings of my youth.
> Then, I watched them from a field.
> Now it's from a city rooftop.
>
> Then and now, the times divide.
> Places differ, here and there.
> Still fluttering alone in the sky,
> that immutable black flag.

Here, the "song" of the sky takes the form of a silent black flag—a symbol of the poet's vague anxiety, perhaps even of himself.

Thirty-four years Chūya's senior, the poet, critic and translator Hōmei Iwano (1873–1920) argued in his *Shintaishi no sahō* (Craft of New Style Poetry, 1907) that Japanese poetry is built on a rhythmic foundation of two, three, and four morae. "Cloudy Sky" follows this approach, written in a segmented style.

Counting the morae in its first four-line stanza, you get 4-3-3-3 / 3-3-5-2 / 4-3-5-3 / 3-4-3-3. Though some fives slip in, the words are deliberately broken into units of two, three, and four.

Hata, the Japanese word for "flag," echoes throughout the poem. Yet, it's a silent resonance: "I couldn't hear the sound."

The second line *hata*, a two-morae word, leads into *hatameku* ("fluttering") to repeat that "hata" sound. It doubles down in the third line's *hata-hata*, crafted so the flag's motion rings as an onomatopoeia—its mute "voice"—in the reader's ear. Even the adverb in the *ima hata* ("now") of the third stanza's fourth line transforms into the flag's flapping sound.

The "song" and "voice" Chūya shape in his poetry, as seen here, echo Hōmei Iwano's attempt to restore the physical rhythm that was lost in Japanese poetic language through its conversion to writing. Additionally, it is important to note that the repetitive sound of the flag fluttering is silent, which makes it the ultimate "song."

We need to grasp this: the "song" and "voice" in Chūya's poetry don't ring out in the real world—they exist only on the page. The silent flapping of the flag in "Cloudy Sky" captures this perfectly.

If this poem were read aloud, expressing that silence would require a physical performance—breaths, pauses, accents—distinct from the world of words. It becomes a different work from one that is realized as written words.

Before "Cloudy Sky," Chūya had already pinned down what makes a poetic "song" succeed in "Dreary Morning," from *Goat Songs*:

> The sound of a shallow stream comes to the mountain.
> Spring light is a stone.
> Water pours from the kakei
> like an old woman reading a story.
>
> Sang, with my isinglass mouth.
> Sang, falling backwards.
> Dry and hoarse, my heart
> walked the tightrope between rocks.

A mysterious fire blazes into the sky!

A deluge of noise crowns me!

• • • • • • • • • • • • • • • • • • • •

Absently, I clap my hands . . .

The "tightrope between rocks" points to Narutaki, a waterfall behind Taizan Temple in Chūya's hometown of Yamaguchi. Ascetics climb its cliff, gripping iron chains that hang from the peak as spray drenches them. The line "Spring light is a stone" is echoed in a moment in "A Fairy Tale" (1936) from *Songs of Bygone Days*: "But the sunlight was something like silica / or an unearthly fine powder." That image appeared here first.

In any case, as the speaker climbs the rocks from which pure white water—as white as an old woman's hair—roars down, he falls backwards while clutching the "rope" and sings. The singing voice is drowned out by the waterfall's roar and cannot be heard. The "song" is in the same state as silence. Or rather, with "A deluge of noise crowns me!" the roar of the waterfall itself becomes the "song." At that moment, the singer's individuality disappears. "Mysterious fire" means just that. Isn't this the ideal state for "song"? That's why the last line applauds it.

To create the structure of a singing voice and the noise that surrounds it, the third, fourth, fifth and sixth stanzas of the six-stanza poem are made into independent lines. Chūya wanted the sound of the waterfall to resonate in those gaps. Moreover, to imagine the sound of the waterfall and the singing voice blending together in equal measures, he needed that fifth stanza made up only of dots (•). It's not a blank or a place to take a breath. He wanted to convey the ultimate in "song" right up until silence.

"It's really far off / but I should wait here," he writes in "Song Without Words" from *Songs of Bygone Days*:

it's really far off
but I should wait here
here the air is faint and dull green
as pale as the roots of a spring onion

I shouldn't be in a rush
should wait here a long time
shouldn't gaze into the distance with virginal eyes
surely I should just wait here

even so it was far away and hazy in the dusk
thick and delicate like the sound of a whistle
but I shouldn't run off in that direction
surely I have to wait here

if I do my panting will settle down
and I can surely get that far
however like chimney smoke
it kept drifting   forever in the crimson sky

What is "it"? Where is "here"? Why must one "wait" for "it"? There is no explanation, but "it" is "far away and hazy in the dusk," has a delicate tone like a distant whistle, and is like chimney smoke "drifting forever in the crimson sky." Moreover, the speaker says, he "shouldn't run off in that direction."

Incidentally, the furigana reading provided for the characters meaning whistle, normally pronounced "gofuki," is "fuitoru," from the Dutch word "fluit," a foreign word that has remained in Yamaguchi since the end of the Edo period. It can also be pronounced "fuitoro" or "fuetoro," which refer to steamship or train whistles. Chūya tossing in local slang here shows how at ease he was when writing this poem.

Let's call "it" "song" for now. The title "Song Without Words" is presumably taken from Verlaine's collection *Romances Sans Paroles*. "It" stays vague on purpose because, in keeping with the title, Nakahara deliberately gave it no words. Better to see "it" as containing the ultimate goal of "song" until it becomes soundless (silence). If "it" within the poem were confined to a single word or defined explicitly, the poem would suddenly shrink into a diminished image. The expansive imagery, which had swelled precisely because what "it" points to was left ambiguous, would wither, and the "song" would slip away.

So, "it" can't be named. "I shouldn't be in a rush/should wait here a long time," he says. In his diary for September 28, 1935, he wrote, "God is in a faraway place, and someday He will grant a name to the confrontation between the mocker and me." Because of that, he says, you may rest easy "here." To "wait" in this "here" is also to preserve the simple essence of life. As the same diary entry puts it: "I am alive — I live vividly — and I live only for the sake of that vivid life."

Chūya would have said: do not analyze or interpret further the question of why we live. "Do not ask me the purpose of my passion!" In this way, Chūya Nakahara's poetry edged toward a music of silence.

Preface

by Christian Nagle

Chūya Nakahara is the most critically discussed Japanese poet in history, and yet, for reasons of circumstance and practicality, he remains almost a complete unknown in the West. He is not alone in this regard, as our ignorance of Japanese poetry extends to most modern and contemporary poets from the Meiji period to the present.

I began translating Chūya (like Danté, he is affectionately called by his first name) in the summer of 1999, during the final year of my doctoral studies in Creative Writing and Literature, when a friend who wanted to introduce me to some modern poets in advance of my emigration to Japan suggested him as a first subject. My language skills were negligible then and I could not read the poems, so, having found no comprehensive editions of Chūya's work in English, we began to compose translations of our own. I was wholly dependent on my friend for producing the rough drafts—basic literalisms that I would then attempt to craft into real poems. It seems to me now that half of my excitement about our endeavors came from the discoveries I was making about the language itself, its grammar, idioms and kanji. Chūya immersed me—with a baptismal shock—in Japanese.

The first translations of Japanese poetry to reach English readers—those of Basil Hall Chamberlain, Ezra Pound and Arthur Waley—were almost exclusively of poems from the Edo period or earlier. These *waka* greatly influenced the work of the Imagist poets who, in turn, became the vanguard of Western poetic Modernism, but no serious efforts were ever made to bring collections of Meiji, Taishō or Shōwa period poetry into English. As late as the 1960s,

Western literati were still cultivating an archaic image of Japanese poetry, with the decade's most important book on the subject being Robert Brower and Earl Miner's *Japanese Court Poetry*, and our tendency to romanticize Japanese poetry as something antiquarian endures to this day in both public and academic realms.

A total of four canonical American poets—Ezra Pound, Kenneth Rexroth, W.S. Merwin, and Gary Snyder—ever translated from the Japanese, and only Snyder did so with fluency. Their efforts produced a volume of work understandably small when compared to the accumulations in other languages, and it is no surprise that, since the dawn of the Taishō period in 1912, a mere five percent of poetry in translation has come from the Japanese, with European languages and Russian accounting for at least eighty. The continued dearth of qualified poet-translators is partly a function of Japanese being an extremely difficult language, combining kanji (ideographs of Chinese origin) with two kana syllabaries (hiragana and katakana) and romaji (Roman characters).

You may therefore feel suspicious of Japanese poetry in translation, approaching it, as many do, under the assumption that its components can have no viable analogs in English. This is what makes haiku anathema to most English-language journals, despite the brave work of Robert Hass: their editors insist that the form requires inclusion of elements carrying no cultural or emotional significance for a Westerner. It's true, the "splash!" of Bashō's frog can't delight in English as it does in Japanese. Yet, the characteristics of court poetry (from which the haiku derives) retained by its inheritors were far more technical than substantive, making a broad understanding of Japan's social and political history unnecessary to enjoying their works. Knowing the national culture will of course add to your reading pleasure, but obscure references need no more in the way of outside research than they would for English-language verse.

Nevertheless, in spite of my attempts to explicate Chūya's

method in the Introduction that follows, some of his poems may strike you as bizarre. But if they sometimes resist easy digestion, you should know that they also do so in the Japanese. His obscurities are not all the result of experimental whim, as even direct cultural and personal references get obfuscated by his maverick style. Who could guess that "The Moon" of *Goat Songs* was inspired by his exposure to Oscar Wilde's *Salomé*, or that the subject of "Deathbed" is a Yokohama prostitute? I therefore include notes at the end of the book that provide some historical, literary and biographical context.

The path to realizing this work was marked by serendipity, beginning with the matching initials of poet and translator. After two years in Japan, with the manuscript in its nascence, I was preparing to return to the US, but decided at the last minute to stay on, with only the vaguest thoughts of completing this volume. A year later, I found myself teaching English at Kōen Girls' School, a private Catholic institution whose most senior Sister, Maria Teresa Chizuko Nishikawa, was Chūya's oldest living relative, and who remembered him from her youth in the 1930s as a moody interloper fixated on her mother, his first cousin, as his Catholic "mentor," despite never having joined the faith himself. The school is located in Kōenji, a district of Tokyo to which, unrelated to Sister Nishikawa's presence there, Chūya moved in 1933, and T-shirts bearing his image can still be found along the shopping promenade. In the school safe, Sister Nishikawa kept a first edition of *Goat Songs*, a volume she once allowed me, in a state of mild stupefaction, to examine. Ultimately, that a few translations executed for fun could have generated a project of so many years seems to me now quite improbable. I can only sign off as Chūya would have, with a shrug and a smirk.

Most important in all this was my being blessed with Yurina Ako, Miyabi Shinadama and Makiko Hayasaka as my assistants. Their acumen, patience and generosity of spirit helped power this work to completion.

I also offer my heartfelt thanks and respects to:

Tuttle co-captains Eric & Christina Oey for your trust, energy and benevolence. You are a binary star in human form, making the world's literary light brighter.

Winnie Bird, my editor, of whose gimlet eye, intuition, empathy and kindness I am unworthy. Your prose is poetry. (Good reader: I recommend to you her wonderful book, *Eating Wild Japan: Tracking the Culture of Foraged Foods.*)

The kaleidoscopic Tuttle team for bringing your skills and optimism to the game.

Mikirō Sasaki, major Japanese poet and the world's leading authority on Chūya. Your Foreword is a hanko representing the greatest literary endorsement this volume could have hoped to receive.

Ambassador Ryōzō Katō, for your compliments, the hours spent discussing diplomacy, literature and baseball, and all those Rhode Island steaks.

Yasuyuki Sugiura, for your unwavering friendship and belief, from our first meeting years ago in Manhattan until today.

Misako Itō, for making this opportunity possible. 永遠に感謝します.

The Nakahara family, for granting me permission to publish these translations.

The editors of the journals where they saw ink.

Dr. Noriko Thunman, for your book, *Nakahara Chūya and French Symbolism*, and your enlightening correspondence.

The Chūya Nakahara Memorial Museum staff for your help with photographs and references.

Fumi Tanakadate and Miki Sugimoto for source materials.

Creative partner Billy Fox, for your unconditional support in the realization of this book.

And my family, parents Dorothy and Chet, brother Chad and sister Susannah, for your love and faith.

Introduction

by Christian Nagle

Who was Chūya Nakahara?

Chūya Nakahara (I follow Western name order throughout this book) died in relative obscurity at the age of thirty, having published only one collection that sold fifty copies. Four years after that insignificant debut, the posthumous *Songs of Bygone Days* was released, and although every poem had found print in his lifetime, the book itself sold under a thousand. However, since the end of World War II, his reputation has grown exponentially, and Chūya is now regarded by many literary critics as the most important figure in the rise of Japanese Modernism. Japanese early modernist poets instituted a number of changes to their art, but by far the most singular of these, as noted by Mikirō Sasaki in his foreword, was replacing literary language with common speech as the idiom of choice. Chūya's work embodies this transformation by incorporating traditional elements of Japanese prosody within free verse. At the same time, his startlingly contemporary voice, complemented by an affinity for Western forms, especially the Petrarchan sonnet, makes him instantly accessible to the Western reader. As such, there exists no better ambassador than Chūya for introducing Japanese early modernist poetry to the West.

Chūya was motivated by conflicting, even paradoxical, impulses: apolitical but fiercely iconoclastic; a progressive formalist; occasional swain of his own urban pastorals; an agnostic singer of prelapsarian hymns. He rejected the language of his age, of any age, striving to articulate what he called "the world before the word," wherein the primeval saturates the sensorial present. He was dismissive of institutions, especially literary schools and scholasticism, because, as he claimed at the start of his career, he was beyond their prescriptions. Yet, for all his bohemian airs—notably the fedora hat and fits of drunken rage—Chūya was a successful autodidact, and his mastery of *waka* (formal Japanese verse) combined with his eventual competency in French to provide the touchstones for his hybrid evolution. He wrote half under the shadow of his Meiji-era predecessors, while straining toward those French Symbolists he admired and translated—Rimbaud, Verlaine, Baudelaire, Mallarmé—and, with an assurance unrivaled by any of his peers, Surrealism. His English, however, was inadequate to an academic understanding of English-language poetry and, like many other Japanese modernists, he was privy only to a random body of English poems in translation, scattered through the journals of his time.

One should not, therefore, consider Chūya in the context of Western poetry. He wrote not within its traditions, only partly out of them. Yet he was, like many other twentieth and twenty-first century Japanese artists, a master of assimilation and transmogrification. Fundamental linguistic and prosodic differences between Japanese, French and English mean that while incorporating whatever formal elements of European poetry he could, Chūya was obliged to make Japanese versions of others. In his sonnets, for example, since Japanese is a language without stressed syllables, he refigures iambic pentameter and alexandrines as *waka*-form lines of 7/5 or 5/7 morae. Although not a pioneer in this regard, Chūya is admired today as one of the most scrupulous pre-war Japanese writers of poems informed by European models. He acquired new thematic and tonal license from the French Symbolists, but the element of their poetry that held the greatest value for him was refrain. Through it he found liberation from the claustrophobic dimensions of tanka and haiku, even while the echoes of their decorum kept his poems grounded in the culture from which they derive.

Chūya's ambivalence to politics and society would almost justify tracing the course of his life apart from the backdrop of national and world events. Still, and despite the brevity of his years, three different emperors ruled during his lifetime: Meiji (1868–1912), Taishō (1912–26) and Shōwa (1926–89). As such, he witnessed some of the most radical socio-political changes in the history of Japan, and however much he lived consciously indifferent to these upheavals, we can better understand his singularity—and the birth of modern Japanese poetry as a whole—through their context.

Chūya and Japanese Early Modernism

The Meiji period was characterized by progress out of chaos. Decades of armed uprisings and factionalism combined with an opening of the country to foreign cultural influences to produce an industrial revolution during which Japan rapidly westernized its infrastructure and established a parliamentary system of government. It was a time of intellectual ferment when socialism's worldwide fervor reached Japan, spawning an urban proletariat whose ideals included welfare, suffrage, and workers' rights. Peaceful protests were put down, violently rose again, and were crushed. The poetry of the era also sought to use Western models to break new ground. *Kanshi* (traditional Japanese poetry) was waning in popularity, and although poet-critic Shiki Masaoka attempted to modernize these lyrics toward more realistic observations of nature, for many literati this amounted merely to putting fresh paint on an old house. They wanted more radical change in the art, and would achieve it through the importation of Western prosody, giving birth to what came to be known as *shintai-shi* (new-style poetry) or *ji-yu-shi* (freestyle poetry). It is generally accepted by Japanese scholars that Modernism in poetry began in 1882 with the publication of *Shintaishi-shō* (Selection of New-Style Poetry), whose authors were three non-poet professors at Tokyo Imperial University who had aspirations in the art. Ironically, in addition to their own work, they included translations of non-contemporary European poets as far back as Shakespeare, but the point of the collection was to create a new Japanese poetry through becoming familiar with the Western canon and following the examples of its greatest poets. By this they meant to throw off the yoke of *waka*, which had ruled the art for centuries with their topical, structural and linguistic constraints, written as they were in literary diction called *bungo* ("boon-go") with prescribed numbers of morae in every phrase. These "delicate fireworks," as one of the collection's authors disparagingly referred to *kanshi*, were to be replaced by a poetry of comprehensive thought written in *kōgo*, or colloquial speech. The public responded with derision, but the stage was now set for a half-century-long revolution in the art, and Chūya himself would often speak of "new-style poetry" and the contributions he felt he was making toward its realization. The next noteworthy collection, *Omokage* (Reflections, 1889), was similar in format to its predecessor, but far superior in quality owing to the fact that its translators—led by Ōgai Mori—were professional writers. Still, the poems' formal rigor was compromised by their stiff *bungo* diction, and the translators, in their attempt to satisfy both modernists and traditionalists, pleased no one in the end. Not until Tōson Shimazaki's *Wakanashū* (Collection of Young Sprouts, 1897), a paean to youth free from feudalistic morality, did a collection of new-style poetry succeed with the general public, in part because the locution was still refined enough to satisfy conservative readers. Among Tōson's contemporaries, the most important of those to achieve any notoriety included Bansui Doi, Kyūkin Susukida and Ariake Kambara, as well as the slightly younger Hakushū Kitahara and Rofū Miki. Miki had read Rimbaud and Verlaine in Bin Ueda's seminal volume of translations, *Kaichōon* (The Sound of Ocean Tides, 1905), and became the first Japanese poet to write in the style of the French *poètes maudits* or "cursed poets," figures closely associated with the Symbolists. It is significant that the last influential collection of the Meiji period included work by foreign poets of which the most contemporary had died only in the preceding decade, for Japan was catching up with the West. By the time of Chūya's birth, it had won wars against both China and Russia to become the pre-eminent power of the Far East, on a nearly equal footing with the US and Europe's colonial monoliths.

Chūya was born on April 29, 1907 to army physician Kensuke Nakahara and his wife Fuku, in the town of Yuda-onsen, Yamaguchi Prefecture, in the western region of Honshu, Japan's main island. The first of six sons, he was pampered as a boy, forbidden to swim with his brothers and neighborhood children, and rarely scolded for misbehavior. His parents continued to spoil him throughout his life with financial support so complete that he was never obliged to seek regular employment, and in poems like "Boyhood" and "Elegy for the Town of Shura" he betrays nostalgia for those carefree early years. Chūya would later become conscious of how such a privileged upbringing shaped his adult character, as he elicited among friends and colleagues almost as much frustration for the obsessive fondness he showed them as for his unpredictability and arrogance.

Chūya was five when the Taishō period began. The Emperor Meiji's successor was of congenitally poor health and lasted only fourteen years, but Taishō Democracy is to this day generally regarded as a time of domestic peace nestled between the wars, between Meiji's turmoil and Shōwa's nationalistic militarism. This was Japan's Jazz Age, an interregnum of prosperity, freedom and cultural exuberance often likened to Weimar Germany or America's Roaring Twenties, although Taishō Japan was not without its internal conflicts, even in the unrestricted realm of poetry. *Sangoshū* (Collection of Coral, 1913), the first important poetry collection of Taishō, was, like the last one of the Meiji era, composed mainly of European poets in translation, but focused heavily on the Symbolists. More talented young poets were now emerging, the most famous being Sakutarō Hagiwara, considered the father of colloquial *kōgo* poetry, but these practitioners of new-style verse were already polarizing into two general camps. One was the proletarian group that wished to give voice to the ideologies of the left that had continued to spread since Meiji, with followers of the major avant-garde movements such as Futurism, Dadaism and Anarchism woven into their ranks; the other was the so-called "artistic" group that admired the Symbolists and espoused a more art-for-art's-sake philosophy. Although Chūya shared aesthetic influences with factions of both groups, namely the Dadaists and Symbolists, he would come to identify more strongly with the latter.

His early promise as a poet is indisputable; Chūya was by any standards a child prodigy. The wellspring of his sensibilities was partly genetic, his father publishing short stories in his spare time as he fantasized about becoming a new Ōgai Mori, the great writer-physician who revolutionized Meiji-period letters while rising to the rank of Surgeon General of the Army Medical Corps. But it was the death from meningitis of his brother Aro (nicknamed Tsugurō) in 1915, when Chūya was eight, that he later identified as providing his first motive to write poetry (in this case, an elegy), and in another three years he was regularly committing tanka to paper. His juvenilia were completely traditional in form and language, but their quality was nonetheless remarkable. Chūya's parents, while coddling their eldest, subjected him to a more strictly disciplined childhood than his younger brothers, but this gave him early academic advantages. Entering Yamaguchi Prefectural Junior High School with excellent test scores in 1920, he at first showed potential for balancing academics and art, but a literary passion gradually overwhelmed him, and his class rank began to suffer. Without his parents' knowledge, he was secretly attending a tanka club called Suguro-no-kai, where he acquired a hunger for both the Japanese canon and foreign works in translation, and learned from the adult attendees how to drink and smoke. That year, at only thirteen, he published tanka in two local newspapers, as well as in a collection entitled *Sugurono* (Spring's Burnt Stubble) with some other young writers. The allure of print was to possess him thereafter until his death.

By this time Taishō Democracy was effectively at an end, the ailing emperor having withdrawn from politics in 1919. His successor Hirohito (Shōwa) was named Prince Regent in 1921, and the ultra-nationalistic faction of government found in him a leader sympathetic to their ideal of a militarized totalitarian state. After the Bolshevik victory in the Russian Civil War the following year, the Comintern sought to rouse the Japanese proletarian movement to revolution, but the government's growing intolerance of leftist groups took an upturn in 1923. Police used the pandemonium following the great earthquake of September 1 to round up labor leaders, Socialists and anyone else deemed anti-establishment, and even murdered some of them, including the anarchist writer and feminist Noe Itō. Three months later a Communist radical made an attempt on Hirohito's life, and the reprisals against leftists—including the writers among them—were widespread and harsh. The arts still flourished, with new sources of inspiration continuing to appear through the import of all things Western, but a conservative trend was taking hold of Taishō artists—as it was all walks of a society that felt it might be losing its identity to foreign influence—and the quake-shaken poets among them began consciously to combine traditional Japanese forms with the European models they had been imitating since Meiji. Some, however, were simply moving with the political tide, sensing that their artistic freedoms were soon to be even more severely curtailed. Chūya himself was still too young and far removed from metropolitan life to be affected by the increasingly stormy political climate, but he was soon to develop into a poet who, while drawing influence as much from writers of the avant-garde as from his *kanshi* forebears, wisely eschewed any overt affiliations, a stance that would make him invisible to the eye of state censorship in the times of political oppression that lay ahead.

Inspiration, Tokyo

In March of 1923, his devotion to letters took its toll when he failed his high school entrance exams, and his embarrassed father sent him away for remedial studies in Kyoto. It is fair to say that the events of the next two years not only brought irrevocable changes in the young man's life, but also determined how its brief balance would be lived. Chūya's poetic style had already been loosening since his arrival in the big city when, in the fall, he discovered Shinkichi Takahashi's *Dadaisuto Shinkichi no Shi* (Poems of the Dadaist Shinkichi, 1923) in a second-hand bookshop. Although this first published collection by a future giant of Japanese letters was in many respects derivative of its European models, its effect on Chūya was profound and permanent, revolutionizing his sense of prosodic and topical possibility. It is no surprise that the earliest of Chūya's own poems that he thought worthy—some would eventually appear in *Goat Songs*—were written in 1924. His habits becoming dissolute, that winter he met his first love, Hiroshima-born Yasuko Hasegawa, a film actress three years his senior who had earned some secondary roles in Tokyo, and the following April they began living together. Also in 1924, Chūya forged his first profound artistic bond, with the poet Tarō Tominaga, a student at the prestigious Kyoto Imperial University, who introduced him to Baudelaire, Rimbaud and the other *poètes maudits*, at first in translation, and later in the original French. Chūya was instantly obsessed and began to compose imitative verse especially akin to Verlaine's in its use of refrain. His life was by now entirely bound up in literature, and so his quitting school (as had Tominaga) in March of 1925 to move to Tokyo with Yasuko seemed inevitable: Chūya later identified August of that year as the time when he decided to devote himself entirely to poetry.

His parents, already at odds with his waywardness, made it conditional to continued financial support that he enroll in a university preparatory school, and although nominally agreeable, he was late getting his papers together for his target schools of Nihon and Waseda. A month after arriving in the capital, he was introduced through Tominaga to the man who was to be most vital to his legacy, Hideo Kobayashi. Although still a student at Tokyo Imperial University, the future king of twentieth century Japanese literary criticism was already distinguishing himself as a writer of influence, and it is germane to his friendship with Chūya that he was himself interested in the Symbolists and music, for both were already vital to Chūya's aesthetic. (Kobayashi would come to owe a great deal of his success as a critic to Baudelaire, whose method he closely studied and copied.) Kobayashi acquainted Chūya with other young literati of Tokyo, including his tutee Shōhei Ōoka, who would go on to become a famous novelist and translator of Stendahl, and ultimately pen a superb Chūya biography. While Chūya both admired and basked in the company of his new artist friends, he quickly became notorious for inciting drunken—sometimes physical—arguments with them, despite (due to his small physical stature) always either losing or, as when he targeted a bemused Ōoka, being allowed to win.

In November, Chūya was struck by two catastrophes: Yasuko left him for Kobayashi, and Tominaga, tired from a long battle with tuberculosis and pleurisy, committed suicide. Although Chūya was devastated by his friend's death, it was the loss of Yasuko that marked the turning point in his maturation as a poet, and critics generally recognize a greater consistency of style in the works written after this date. Indeed, he seemed almost to be announcing his debut to himself when in May of 1926 he wrote the sonnet "Morning Song," universally recognized as one of his finest poems. Still, his art provided no relief from the mortification of his heart, and Chūya visited Yasuko and Kobayashi obsessively until the couple finally fled from Tokyo to escape him. He enrolled in the Literature Department of Nihon University, but soon dropped out to focus on his writing. To the coterie magazine *Yamamayu* (Mountain Co-

coon), with which Tominaga and Kobayashi were both associated, he contributed the essay "Tominaga's Premature Death," the first work he published in the capital.

The late 1920s saw Chūya's reputation as a Tokyo poet solidifying, aided as it was by an expanding literary network. In 1928, Chūya brought "Morning Song" and "Deathbed" to Tetsutarō Kawakami, one of Kobayashi's fellow literary critics and a pianist in the modernist musical group Surya ("Sun God" in Sanskrit), asking him to set them to music. Kawakami introduced Chūya to the leaders, Saburō Moroi and Seiichirō Utsumi, who scored the poems, and in May the group performed them. The structure of these poems lent themselves readily to song: one is a sonnet, the other a sonnetesque sixteen-liner, and both are wrought in regular morae and utilize Symbolist-style repetition, which made them composer and singer-friendly as lyrics. That same month Kobayashi broke up with Yasuko, and while this did not affect his relationship with Chūya, the latter took it as a cue to renew his pursuit of the actress, a hopeless endeavor that would last for another year and a half. Also in May, Chūya's father died at the age of fifty-two, but his mother Fuku, concerned about public opinion, did not allow Chūya to return for the funeral. (Having collapsed in March, Kensuke reportedly cried as he read "Morning Song" and "Deathbed" while on his own deathbed in hospital.) In 1929, Chūya and Kawakami co-founded *Hakuchigun* (Band of Idiots), a coterie magazine centering on French literature, with Kawakami serving as editor. Ōoka, and Rokurō Abe, to whom "Sinner's Song" is dedicated, were also on the masthead. The name was chosen as an homage to Dostoyevsky, whom Kobayashi revered, and also to mock the Japanese bourgeoisie's general view of artists. Besides the many future luminaries who contributed work was the mysterious Sakiko Kobayashi, nom de plume for Yasuko, who had, on Chūya's insistence—clearly as a pretext for making regular contact with her—tried her hand at both poetry and prose. Perhaps due to the dual motivations of his editorial position and a desire to impress Yasuko, Chūya worked with an enthusiasm he showed toward no other magazine, but *Hakuchigun*'s run would be over in a year after only six issues. In May the ex-lovers traveled to Kyoto together, but Yasuko was by this time involved with theater director Yukiyo Yamakawa, and Chūya was unable to rekindle their romance. He spent the rest of the year focused on publishing his own work, including translations, in various journals.

Maturation

With Shōwa's succession to the throne, militarist Japan acquired broader recognition as a world power. Still, its government enjoyed only questionable success in both domestic and foreign policy, as it sought both to enforce national unity through harsh public security laws and expand its interests in China. Hostility toward politically marginal groups intensified, with subversive writers now coming under direct scrutiny of the Tokkō (Special Higher Police), and many of them were rounded up in the March 15 Incident of 1928, imprisoned, and forced to recant. In 1930 began a two-year period of social upheaval known as the Shōwa Crisis, during which thousands of social conflicts and even outright revolts erupted, in spite of the state's extremely repressive measures. But in the wake of the Manchurian Incident of 1931, staged as a pretext to invade China, the government forcibly and finally dissolved both the Japanese Communist Party and the proletarian literature movement. Suspect professors were removed from faculties as prestigious as Tokyo Imperial University. By the early 1930s the last voices of subversion had been silenced, and Japan found itself politically isolated as international condemnation of its puppet state of Manchukuo led to its withdrawal from the League of Nations.

Chūya coasted through these years of persecution with diffident ease. His outspokenly nonpartisan mindset, confirmed by the content of his work and the absence of political commentary in his diary and notebook, served him well: with a style that utilized Dadaism's techniques but did not recognize the movement's radical leftist connections, he was never considered a threat by the establishment, nor arrested, except for drunk and disorderly conduct. While many writers, including his friend Kobayashi, would succumb to fear of persecution (and unemployment) and begin to churn out propagandistic works defending Japan's policy of Pan-Asian subjugation, Chūya remained authentically indifferent to events in the game of nations.

April of 1930 saw the publication of *Hakuchigun*'s final number, and although half of the issue was devoted to Chūya—ten poems and an essay entitled "A Discussion of Poetry"—he was heartbroken by the journal's demise, which cast him adrift in Tokyo for a second time. A welcome boost soon followed when Surya set to music and performed more of his poems. In September, finally honoring the behests of Fuku, on whose stipends he was dependent, he entered Chūō University's preparatory school, although his tenure there was short-lived. His colleagues provided him with even more professional inspiration, Kobayashi by publishing the first Japanese translation of Rimbaud's *Une saison en enfer* (*A Season in Hell*) with reputable publishing house Hakusuisha, and poet Tatsuji Miyoshi with his *Sokuryōsen* (Survey Vessel), a daring collection that attempted to engage the entire spectrum of possibility in modern poetry. But then in December, Yasuko gave birth to an illegitimate son. Chūya not only became the godfather, but named the boy and lavished him with affection as though he were his own. But this spelled the symbolic end to any possibility of reconciliation and, taken together with the failure of the magazine, the final loss of Yasuko hurt Chūya so badly that he could write nothing for months. In April 1931, while still loosely tethered to Chūō, he immersed himself in the Athénée Français, a French-language school within the Tokyo School of Foreign Languages. His aim was to qualify to become a diplomatic secretary in France—not for any interest in being a part of the government abroad, but simply as an opportunity to live for a time in the homeland of his poetic heroes. He would ultimately finish his studies but abandon the plan. In September, his brother Kōzo died of pulmonary tuberculosis, and Chūya traveled home to see his face one last time before he was cremated.

In the spring of 1932 he compiled a provisional version of his first collection, *Yagi no uta* (*Goat Songs)*, and by April was editing it with a mind for publication. Yet, although the forty-four-poem manuscript contained many published works and some of his masterpieces, the houses to which he submitted all considered it too diverse and uneven to merit a run, and Chūya was obliged to resort to a vanity pressing. His two summer subscription notices garnered only ten signatures (his friends denied him out of concern that he would spend the proceeds on alcohol), but a donation from his mother funded a press run covering two hundred copies, and *Goat Songs* was released in December with no fanfare, although Kobayashi and others recognized its importance.

Chūya sought to put Yasuko behind him once and for all through marriage, and in January 1933 he proposed to Mutsuko Sakamoto—a beautiful young Ginza hostess much desired in his literary circle and the model for Ōoka's novel *Kaei* (The Shade of Blossoms)—but was rejected. His mother then hired a matchmaker, who arranged his courtship of Takako Ueno, a distant cousin six years his junior. For one as committed as Chūya to replicating the bohemian decadence of his Symbolist heroes, submitting to such a conservative institution as matchmaking seems incongruous, but the wishes of his mother-financier won out, and he married Takako on December third. Chūya would in fact embrace domesticity with an enthusiasm that betrayed a desire to escape both his romantic failures and idiosyncratic waywardness. Although still supported by stipends from home, he had become more serious about his work since meeting Takako, publishing poems in the magazines *Shiki* (Four Seasons) and *Kigen* (Era), some of which would appear posthumously in *Songs of Bygone Days*. Just a week after his marriage, his long-awaited breakthrough came when brand new publishing house Mikasa Shobō put out a volume of his translations entitled *Ranbō shishū (gakkō jidai no shi)* (Rimbaud: Poems of School Days). It was a lasting critical success, with Japanese and French scholars to this day in agreement that any errors in detail are more than compensated by Chūya's realization of Rimbaud's ésprit.

Final Years and Legacy

To remind the reader of a point made by Mikirō Sasaki in his Foreword, the word "tragedy" derives from the Greek *tragoidia*, which is a compound of *tragos* or "goat" and *odí*, meaning "song"—a fact that, however darkly fortuitous, is appropriate to Chūya. His legacy as a tragic figure derives not merely from his early death, but the fact that he died so soon after having finally achieved, in the last four years of his life, a degree of stability and happiness. In 1934 he began to write prose regularly again, resuming in earnest his journal, whose entries had become sporadic. His first son, Fumiya, was born in October, and a photograph of him smiling at the baby in his arms confirms the reportage, including Chūya's own, of his profound happiness at becoming a father. The next year, Chūya found himself enjoying regular publication of his poems and translations, including contributions to the magazine published by *Rekitei*, a literary coterie at whose meetings he also gave memorable readings. Noted Shimpei Kusano in the Chūya memorial issue of *Bungakukai* (Literary World): "His readings lived up to what people call 'original' . . . His character, poems and readings were inseparable." In his diary for July, Chūya made the following optimistic, though odd, entry: "Bequeathed item—I hope Fumiya will like poetry. I believe we could do quite a lot in two generations." His words proved fatal though, as the tubercular cloud (more romantic followers might say the curse) that had followed him since his youth again descended on someone close to him, and Fumiya fell ill, dying in November, just a month after his second birthday. This tragedy was one from which Chūya seemed never to recover. He did not sleep or leave the child's side for three days, and eventually had a nervous breakdown. The December birth of his second son Yoshimasa offered a flicker of light but could not console him. He began to suffer from auditory hallucinations, arguing with phantoms, and to behave regressively, alarming Takako enough to call for Fuku, who, in January of 1937, checked him into Nakamura Kokyō Sanatorium in Chiba, east of Tokyo.

Chūya stayed there until mid-February and despite his grief wrote prolifically—poems, essays and letters, as well as an account of his treatment. He returned home upon his release, but, haunted by Fumiya's ghost in every room, quickly moved with his family to the coastal refuge of Kamakura, a hub for literati where Kobayashi, Ōoka, and others were already living. Although again exhausted by September, he managed to finish editing his second volume, *Arishi hi no uta* (Songs of Bygone Days), which he dedicated to Fumiya and then, perhaps sensing his own death was near, entrusted to Kobayashi, along with all his uncollected manuscripts. That same month, his *Ranbō shishū (*Selected Poems of Rimbaud) was published by Noda Bookstore. After thirteen years of living elsewhere, Chūya began making plans to move back to his Yamaguchi hometown, but became ill with an appetite disorder (possibly a symptom of brain damage from tubercular infection), which he tried to assuage with alcohol. In early October his condition worsened, and he was again hospitalized. On the twenty-first Yasuko and her new businessman husband visited him, but by then Chūya was delirious. The next day, after becoming lucid for a brief period during which he insisted to his mother that he was a "loyal son"—a declaration that would prove financially true—he died of tuberculous meningitis. Yoshimasa followed him into death only three months later.

Chūya was a Japanese poet as defined by his language and the literary traditions he was helping both to uphold and transform. Like many of his quasi-revolutionary contemporaries, he was fond of making universal proclamations about poetry, these born perhaps of a relativistic despair that the Continental experiment would succeed, as it did, without him. Yet, unlike many of them, Chūya would never succumb to the limitations of manifesto, remaining a maverick presence at the salons to which he lent his voice, and in their spirited, fleeting magazines. His intense, private industry seems an almost disdainful response to the Japanese "group society" mindset, but it resulted in an oeuvre and artist now revered as distinctly Japanese. Still, Chūya's biography leads one to think of certain Western poets whose early demise also spawned cult followings, popularity that far exceeded what they had enjoyed in life: John Keats, Sylvia Plath, and of course Rimbaud. While his death hardly registered in a country feverish with military nationalism, Kobayashi pushed *Songs of Bygone Days* into print in 1938, laying the groundwork for Chūya's postwar acclaim. Even so, not even his greatest admirers could have predicted his eventual status in Japanese letters, established in 1947 when war-shattered and penniless Japan bought over twenty thousand copies of a new Chūya collection. Interest in his unpublished poems and drafts has continued at a peak ever since, and the definitive version of his collected works spans six volumes. The poet who had always relied on his parents' charity to survive became an extraordinary success after death, as a nonstop windfall of royalties from his book sales helped to sustain Fuku and other family members for the rest of their lives.

Translating Chūya

Chūya offers the poet-translator some unique challenges in content and form. His idiom is comprehensible and surprisingly modern, but he can blend anachronism, neologism, onomatopoeia, song and surreal oddity with such freedom that at times his lines are puzzling even to the keenest scholars. This is further complicated by the fact that common-use kanji were simplified by the Japanese government after World War II: pre-war Japanese is fraught with antiquities that sometimes require a kind of double translation—first into contemporary Japanese, and then into English—before an appropriate equivalent can be identified. Such an environment makes compromise inevitable, yet in all the years I spent working on the poems in this book, the text never resisted me to the extent that I was obliged to do violence to the original. In any case, Chūya's formal concerns are so varied and particular that I should take time here to discuss my approach to each.

Line and Punctuation

As novelist Michael Cunningham once said, "Japanese and English have different physics," and this is most immediately and significantly evident in the realignment of Japanese text for Western readerships, as in this volume, from vertical/right-to-left order to horizontal/left-to-right. In reading a Japanese poem in the original, one feels a bodily communion with the text, each line being synchronous with a single exhalation, and this sensation is absent in English (unless one is reading Allen Ginsberg's "Howl"). Not so different from its Western equivalents, however, are Japanese punctuation marks. The *kuten* (。) is generally used in the same way as our period in that it separates consecutive sentences, although it is not always found when the end of a sentence is otherwise obvious, as with lines that stand alone or close a stanza. The Japanese comma or *tōten* (、) indicates the junction of two phrases or sentences, and suggests a place for the reader to pause or breathe. Even when a line of poetry doesn't end with one, it is to be read in a single breath.

For Taishō Japan, Western punctuation marks such as the ellipsis, dash, exclamation point and asterisk were recent acquisitions from Europe, but even if Chūya knew the rules for their usage in English, he clearly cared little about emulating them in Japanese.

In fact, his usage often seems like affectation, the self-conscious role-playing of a poet keen to be perceived as an international. He even invents his own punctuation mark—the heavy midline dots one finds in "Dreary Morning," "Autumn" and "Korean Woman." Yet, such gestures were surely born of the same motivation as his use of foreign words in both katakana and the original languages, or the deft Matisse-like pencil sketches that populate his notebooks. Chūya deployed these new symbols not as gratuitous experimentalism but with intent, seeing in them an opportunity to expand his already daring range of expression. He was "riffing," as they say in the jazz world. Improvising. The asterisks in "Rainy Day" are representative in this regard, with what might appear to be idiosyncratic whim in fact serving the gestalt of the piece. Some poems are not punctuated at all, others only half so ("Autumn News" and "Skylarks" contain not a single *kuten*), and still others oddly, at least to Western eyes, full of apparent "comma splices," since Chuya's *tōten* variously do the equivalent work of em-dash, ellipsis, colon, semicolon and even period. The reader will therefore forgive, I hope, my making substitutions in, and additions or deletions of, punctuation when it is essential to preserving the sense of the original. His dashes are a special case. For, while Chūya would have understood their Western typographical function from the countless French works he had read, he does not use them to make syntactic pivots or offset clauses. Instead, as in "Elegy for the Town of Shura" and elsewhere, he draws them at the beginning and end of lines, even after a *tōten* or *kuten*, so that they manifest, like those of Emily Dickinson, as glyphs more relevant to the poem's rhythm and physicality—as well as his own psychology—than syntax. As such, I preserved as many of them as I could, even when they are at odds with Western convention. Finally: where Chūya mostly or entirely omits punctuation ("Homecoming," "Tree Shade," "Skylarks," "The Village Clock"), I do the same, resulting in a poem devoid of capital letters; however, where he implies complete sentences and the English analog would otherwise read awkwardly, I take the liberty of structuring it with punctuation ("Shame," "Autumn Day Madness," "Korean Woman," "Single").

Technique

Chūya was a rigorous craftsman who combined elements of Japanese and Western poetry with increasing assurance throughout his brief career. Into his well-wrought structures he poured an audacious blend of *kango* (ancient Chinese), *wago* (native Japanese) and *gairaigo* (Western words), such as we might liken to the polyglot fireworks of Ezra Pound in his *Cantos*, though perhaps with fewer errors. The poems exhibit a high volume of *waka*-like phrases, and these are especially evident in his more formal pieces such as the sonnets, which are informed by French models. Since he acquired enough skill in French to recognize that its prosody differs from Japanese primarily in being accentual, the sonnet offers an ideal site wherein to discover what Chūya felt to be the appropriate Japanese equivalent to loosened iambic meter: regular morae phrases of 7/5, with 8, 6 and 4 variations. It is perhaps fair to infer by inversion that, were Japanese accentual, Chūya would have been writing accentual-syllabic verse, since that would have been the primary mode of his nineteenth century forebears. I should point out that, unless one is using honorifics, Japanese generally takes up less space than English—but the regular phonemic counts in Chūya's poems are a prosodic concern that can be satisfied quite naturally, even while retaining an awareness of the iamb, as with the closing 5/7 tercets of the sonnet "Morning Song," which I render into a 7-syllable line followed by a 5/5 and another 7. Often, his 7/5s and 8/6s resolve naturally into iambic pentameter—loosened, as in the first six lines of "The Moon" from Goat Songs, or perfect, as in this line from "Portrait of a Certain Man": *Appearing at the café every night.* Generally, whenever Chūya writes with a consciousness of *waka*, I use iamb-based line substitutions arranged into phrases that reflect his "syllabics." In this way, and like the *Omokage* translators, who found *waka* equivalents to Western prosodic conventions, I hope to retain something of the East-West hybrid element that makes them unique. Chūya seldom divides the Japanese metrical phrases as explicitly as he does in "Morning Song," where the breaks manifest as physical spaces that, more than mere caesuras, represent the speaker's waking consciousness, or as he does in another sonnet, "Summer," where it seems the speaker's tubercular coughing hampers the poem's coherence. Usually the breaks are implied by the grammar (Japanese is closer in structure to Korean and Turkish than English), which gives the translator a commensurate flexibility in merging phrases.

Still, for all Chūya's formal particularity, the two most common descriptors associated with his poetry are "music" and "rhythm" (his prose manifests these qualities as well). That he should have found such inspiration from music is surprising in one who couldn't play an instrument, but contrary to his apparently chagrined attitude in "Voice of Life," he adored classical and jazz, and listened constantly to LPs with friends and colleagues. He believed, like his Japanese forebears, in the sung quality of poetry. Let me here make a distinction between the kanji for "poem" (詩) and "song" (歌). The former originally referred to classical Chinese poetry and later extended to Modern free verse, conveying a more literary, written tradition; the latter refers to Japanese lyrical forms like *waka* and *tanka*, which were meant to be sung or chanted. Thus, Chūya's exclusive use of 歌 in his poem titles is significant. He worked constantly to manifest music in his verse, and it is natural that progressive composers from his own period until today have found his poetry so well-suited to scoring. He had a fine ear and a penchant for singing his own poems, varying his delivery and speech patterns to distinguish their various characters. As a former professional choral singer/jazz and rock composer who worked on these translations with assistants who hold higher degrees in music, I feel optimistic that some justice has been done to this very important aspect of Chūya's work. Absent melodies, though, what does "music" mean with regard to poetry?

Refrain and Repetition

In Chūya's case, it is surely the libretto-like quality of his poems: many both look and read like song lyrics, with refrains that are sometimes composed of whole verses as in "Hangover," "Tree Shade," "New Year's Eve Bell" and "Moonlit Beach." Of greater interest to musicians, however, will be the poems like "Memory," wherein Chūya spins variations on refrains in the same way John Coltrane would deconstruct chords in his solos, playing note-by-note versions of them until he had exhausted all possibilities. This kind of music shares a co-dependency with rhythm, recombining as they do in a complex of aural and visual elements, and I shall discuss each in turn.

Since all but one of the forty-six basic morae of Japanese ends in a vowel sound, its poetry is not conscious of rhyme (as with Italian, it is nearly impossible *not* to rhyme), but Chūya was nevertheless intentionally repeating certain phonemes at the ends of, within and across lines. This is easily observed in "Image," where every line ends with one of six syllabic hiragana characters – き/た/ひ/と/く/で (ki/ta/hi/to/ku/de) in the first section and に/く/り/き/や/す (ni/ku/ri/ki/ya/su) in the second—and these morae can also be found within lines throughout the piece. The same internal consciousness is evident in all of the poems in this volume. As such, I avoid perfect rhymes in my translations, trying instead to unify the poems with networks of slant rhymes, often internal, in the hopes that the accumulation will be more felt than heard, for this is how the Japanese affects the native reader.

As noted above, Chūya's repetitions are sometimes simply refrains, a recurring phrase, line or stanza, but more often they manifest as song-like utterances at line endings or grammatical tags that have no literal English equivalents. When I encounter these, I usually try to imply correspondence between the lines through other means, such as slant rhyme, assonance, consonance or meter. In the second stanza of the second section of "Autumn," the Japanese lines all end with "ね" (ne), a monosyllabic suffix that acts like a request for affirmation. In conversational Japanese, it is so ubiquitous as to carry only subtle significance, whereas the closest English equivalent—"right?"—has a too-tangible presence that, if repeated, would make the speaker sound like someone with a compulsive verbal tick. So, since the "ね" here serves primarily to offset the two speakers' rhythms, I stole a page from T.S. Eliot's "The Four Quartets" and employed falling meter, ending each line with an unstressed syllable, thus binding the lines of the first speaker more subtly, through repetition of a stress pattern rather than a word.

Most intriguing, perhaps, is Chūya's repetition of kanji, for this reveals the figures around which he is conjuring his meditations. It is sometimes a simple case of characters reappearing verbatim, but he also repeats certain components by deploying kanji that variously contain them. In "Twilight," moon (月), sun/day (日), eye (目) and stand (立) appear as elements of such kanji as those in the title, 黄昏, 暗 (gloom), 面 (surface), 音 (sound), 明 (brightness), 見 (see), 竟 (at last), 親 (parent) and 映像 (image). Many of these are connected as members of word families, others only by apparent coincidence, yet Chūya's complete oeuvre shows that he was keenly aware of how his poems appeared on the page, that he wished to craft tapestries whose visual manifestations reflected their aural and linguistic coherence: to the native reader's eye, his poems look as attractive as they sound. An even more elaborate example is the sonnet-like "Sigh," wherein Chūya weaves the following network: the left-side kanji appear either as free-standing characters, components (sometimes only visual) of the more complex kanji on the right, or both:

Kanji	Meaning	Component of
日	sun/day	瘴, 者, 間, 響, 原, 音, 層
立	stand/set	瘴, 響, 音, 端, 瞳, 帝
田	field	町, 野, 瞳, 層, 魚
白	white	線, 百, 原, 蝗
中	middle	仲, 蝗, 螽
土	earth	野, 瞳, 遠
目	eye/care/class	瞬, 瞳, 看
穴	hole/cave	窓, 突, 空
ム	self	窓, 響, 曇
小	small	線, 原, 叔
夕	evening	瞬, 怨
門	gate	間, 開
心	heart/mind	怨, 窓
雨	rain	雲, 曇

You will notice a good deal of overlap in the above. Many of the complex kanji include multiple basic kanji from the left margin, like 瞳 (pupil), which includes the four characters 目, 立, 田 and 土. It must be said that many basic kanji are commonly found as components of the thousands of kanji in general use, but lest you suspect this list to be the product of wishful thinking or coincidence, remember that there are often multiple kanji possibilities available to convey the same idea, especially in pre-war letters. Chūya could have used the more basic 目 to represent "eye," but cross-references are useful to this surreal landscape, and with 瞳 he creates resonance between the locust eyes and fourteen other kanji instead of just four. Moreover, a poet also always has the option of "spelling out" a kanji syllabically, in kana, as Chūya does strategically throughout his two books, dispensing with the gravity of Chinese characters in favor of a less overtly integrated, more colloquial quality. This may be seen in the very title of this poem, where he substitutes the inappropriately dense kanji for "sigh" (溜息) with the lighter hiragana ためいき. The best confirmation of Chūya's conscious manipulation of this poem's physicality lies in how often he repeats components of the kanji for Tetsutarō Kawakami (河上徹太郎), to whom "Sigh" is dedicated. They are found in no less than twenty kanji across fourteen lines—沼, 若, 深, 石, 荷 (twice), 覗 (twice), 行, 松, 私, 叔, 曇, 雲, 窓, 大, 突, 蝗, 瞳, 響—so that, like a multi-dimensional acrostic, the name is everywhere in the poem. All of which is to suggest that the reader illiterate in Japanese may nonetheless take pleasure in the physicality of the original poems: one need not understand the meanings of the kanji to appreciate how Chūya combines them to effect.

Finally, a word must be said about Chūya's mostly non-repeating kanji and their impact on the poetry. Those that begin lines—what I call "head characters"—are the most important, and are the analog for end-words in English poetry. Choose any poem in this book and run your eyes down the first and last characters of each line: you will notice a preponderance of kanji on the left and a like proportion of simpler kana on the right. Of the fourteen lines in the sonnet "Autumn Day," thirteen begin with kanji and thirteen end with kana, which is indicative of the lines having a left-side (or, in the original, a high) center of gravity, but it is the balance of kanji and kana throughout that determines the weight, speed and tone of the poem as whole. Most kanji are visually complex and pronounced with two or three morae (although they can contain up to five), so the eyes must hover over the character as it is read, thus slowing the pace. Their complexity also carries both a physical and psychological weight: they connote seriousness and maturity; to process them requires education; foreign students often regard them as lexicographic puzzles, and there is a feeling of code or acronym about them. In the realm of poetry, they hearken to *bungo*, or classical Japanese verse. By comparison, kana are single-morae phonemes over which the eyes move briskly. In kindergarten, children learn to spell their first words with kana equivalents of kanji before beginning their ten-year kanji studies course, which lends kana a "lighter" quality, more reminiscent of *kōgo*. It must be noted that, unlike Chinese, not all Japanese words even have an ascribed kanji: many are written only in hiragana (or, if the word was adopted from a foreign language, katakana), but a writer always has the option, as with ためいき, of spelling the kanji out in hiragana. Again, the meaning of the characters is separate from a poem's physiology, which empowers a craftsman like Chūya to control the quality of the language from line to line through combinations of kana and kanji. With regard to Japanese head characters and English end words, it is worth adding that this equivalence, combined with the fact that Japanese syntax is mostly unlike that of English, with main verbs at the end, means that line breaks and their occasional surprises will differ. Chūya does not, for example, employ the Western device of separating a modifier from a noun across a line break—surely the influence of *waka* tradition. I have done my best to respect his formalism in this regard, while remaining conscious of how his often strict "syllabics" can accommodate what is pleasing and idiomatically natural in English.

Chūya's Style

Armed with an understanding of Chūya the technician, one may still be at a loss over how to characterize Chūya the stylist. That remains a subject of lively discussion among literary scholars to this day, and the challenges that attend deciphering him only deepen with the language gap. All translators face the same conundrum of reconciling the literal with the idiomatic. Those with minimal knowledge of the source language make themselves woefully dependent on their native assistants, and their work tends toward loose renderings that capture word-for-word meaning while neglecting idiom and prosody. Even those with command of the foreign language may allow themselves liberal interpretations of the original works in the name of "doing the artist justice" in the new tongue.

The best of these sometimes pen definitive versions. But the true masters are those who transcend the easy binary, and here I think of my late teacher and friend Richard Howard, whose translation of Baudelaire's *Les Fleurs du mal* (*Flowers of Evil*) earned him The Medal of Honor from the French Academy, which praised it for its balance of accuracy and poetic sensibility. As one whose second language is French and who began studying the French canon at a young age, I can only concur: they are spiritually inspired works to whose brilliance any translator should aspire. Where Chūya is concerned, I have refused to take license with the language when the poet has made clear choices in diction. Until the Japanese government introduced the Tōyō Kanji list after World War II, reducing the number of kanji required for general education from over 10,000 to around 2,000, the language included a vast array of specialized characters, many of them drawn from classical Chinese. Thus, although perhaps not as expansive as pre-war English, Taishō Japanese comprised a huge vocabulary, and Chuya's personal word bank was massive, owing in substantial part to his having studied centuries of *waka*. Once I acquired a literal reading of a poem, therefore, my interpretive task was largely one of finding English-language analogs for how the poet's perceptive singularity forges meaning through his technical kaleidoscope and that most interculturally elusive element, tone.

Ultimately, I lack the space here to digest the countless volumes of criticism on the subject of Chūya's style, and it would not be useful to Western readers if I did so, since this would inevitably lead to comparisons, and most would be unfamiliar with any of the Japanese poets in whose tradition Chūya is thought to have written. As for Western correlatives, we may find Chūya reminding us variously of Christina Rossetti and Hardy in exactitude, Pound in fragmented imagery, Rilke and Stevens in philosophical discursiveness, Moore in impish irony, and Hopkins in his use of neologism, wordplay and onomatopoeia. But there is little value in noting such similarities, for the bard of Yamaguchi neither read nor was influenced by any of these poets (save, perhaps, Rossetti and Rilke), and the bulk of those to whom he was exposed were represented only by isolated poems, cobbled together in arbitrary anthologies that offered little in the way of literary or historical context. The source languages of these works, moreover, were confined to Western Europe, leaving Chūya unaware of Russian, Polish and Spanish writers, as well as those from the Americas and other countries of Eastern Europe. Still, although he also knew his Symbolist heroes mostly in abstract, severed from the broader currents of French and Continental literature, they offered catalyst enough to ignite his revolution, and Chūya, with his bohemian affectations, pays explicit homage to them in ways that provide a clear roster of his canonical models.

Nevertheless, to call him, as did Takaaki Yoshimoto, "the Japanese Rimbaud," an idea underscored by other critics, is to draw an analogy so neat as to do disservice to both poets. For although enamored of and maturing almost as early as the *enfant terrible* of Charleville, and while provided with a backdrop of sufficient upheaval to justify assuming the social disaffection of the *poètes maudits*, Chūya's passion for the art never extended, as did theirs, beyond the language of literary and personal history. Ironically, he did suffer an early death like Baudelaire and Rimbaud. But if he did, however unconsciously (or amusingly, as in "Autumn"), predict or will his own demise, it would serve as confirmation to those who believe his persona was something of a construct—as is, surely, that of every artist, including Rimbaud, who explicitly articulated a plan to fashion himself into a seer. Still, as a child of privilege who suffered none of his French idols' financial hardships; who, despite his alcoholism, could not imagine the physical ruin wrought upon them by their addictions to laudanum and absinthe, and as one whose art was ignored in his lifetime, not once precipitating scandal, let alone condemnation, Chūya, for all his efforts, could never hope to suffer as had the Symbolists. In dying young, however, he paid them the ultimate compliment of imitation, leaving a legacy that would rival theirs in tragedy.

In attempting to situate a writer in the context of period as well as the greater arc of national literature, the field of literary criticism generally depends on ideas regarding inheritance and succession. It tells us that there might have been no Wordsworth without Thomas Gray, no H.D. without Sappho. Such tidy pairings may be useful as a gateway to poetic history, but they are at best a convenience that cannot hope to bind together the myriad threads of its tapestry. After all, poets have been copying and stealing from each other since the Epic of Gilgamesh was first carved in clay. Eliot spoke succinctly to the question in *The Sacred Wood: Essays on Poetry and Criticism*: "Immature poets imitate; mature poets steal; bad poets deface what they take, and good poets make it into something better, or at least something different." During the decade in which Chūya developed, the 1920s, began a phenomenon that was to continue through the twentieth century, that of Japanese artists in all mediums imitating their Western counterparts and being subsequently criticized as lacking in originality, depth and soul. Setting aside the irony that the forebears of Western poetic Modernism, the Imagists, had taken inspiration from classical Japanese poetry, such a generalization is still too simple, for on closer examination we invariably find that the Japanese artist has not merely assimilated but, with the addition of native ingredients, transmogrified the foreign thing into something very much their own. We need look no further than the culinary arts as a paradigm: it is the application by Tokyo chefs of the complex subtleties that characterize their native cuisine to imports like tempura, ramen and hamburgers over the years that has made theirs the finest restaurant city in the world.

So it was with Chūya. Using *waka* as a foundation, he was at first an exuberant if imitative experimentalist, fashioning poems after the Dadaists and Symbolists as a means of discovery, but these

Western models served as no more than a springboard to launch his unique, burgeoning voice. He was incredibly prolific, and we should remember that these two books represent only what he (and his trusted peers) believed would make the most cohesive manuscripts in 1934 and 1938 respectively. Every writer has experienced Chūya's agony in having to kill so many of their darlings—superb pieces that simply didn't fit. He produced hundreds more poems, most of them unpublished, as well as countless prose works and letters, and to survey his complete oeuvre is to understand that, even while still a teenager, Chūya had already developed beyond the penumbra of imitation into the living embodiment of his own poetry. He was a one of one. Whatever sensational effects he initially employed became subsumed in the greater aesthetic of a mature young genius, and his work is today revered in the scholarship as wholly original, Chūya himself as the purest Japanese poet of the twentieth century.

Sources

Brower, Robert H., and Earl Miner. *Japanese Court Poetry.* Stanford, CA: Stanford University Press, 1961.

Dolin, Alexander. *The Bronze Age of Japanese Poetry: The Surge of Modern Verse in the Meiji–Taishō–Early Shōwa Period.* Akita City: Akita International University Press, 2015.

Dumas, Raechel. "The Aesthetics of Transcendence: Nakahara Chūya and the Poetics of Japanese Modernity." *South Atlantic Review* 76, no. 4 (Fall 2011): 155–169.

Katō, Shūichi. *A History of Japanese Literature.* Translated by David Chibbett. 3 vols. Tokyo: Kodansha International, Ltd, 1979–1983.

Kawamoto, Kōji. *Nihon Shiika no Dentō: Nana to Go no Shigaku.* Tokyo: Iwanami Shoten, 1991.

Keene, Donald. *Dawn to the West: Japanese Literature of the Modern Era—Poetry, Drama, Criticism.* New York: Holt, Rinehart and

Winston, 1984.

———. *Seeds in the Heart: Japanese Literature from Earliest Times to the Late Sixteenth Century.* New York: Henry Holt & Co., 1993.

———. *The Pleasures of Japanese Literature.* New York: Columbia University Press, 1988.

Konishi, Jin'ichi. *A History of Japanese Literature. Vol. 1, The Archaic and Ancient Ages.* Edited by Earl Miner. Translated by Aileen Gatten and Nicholas Teele. Princeton, NJ: Princeton University Press, 1984.

Naganuma, Mitsuhiko. *Nakahara Chūya no Jidai.* Tokyo: Kasama Shōin, 2011.

Nakamura, Minoru. *Nakahara Chūya: Kotoba Naki Uta.* Revised ed. Tokyo: Chikuma Shobō, 1990.

Ōoka, Shōhei. *Nakahara Chūya.* Tokyo: Kadokawa Shoten, 1974.

Sasaki, Mikirō, et al., eds. *Shinpen Nakahara Chūya Zenshū.* Tokyo: Kadokawa Shoten, 2004.

Sasaki, Mikirō. *Nakahara Chūya—Chinmoku no Ongaku.* Tokyo: Iwanami Shoten, 2017.

Satō, Yasumasa. *Nakahara Chūya to Iu Basho.* Tokyo: Shichōsha, 2008.

Shirane, Haruo, Tomi Suzuki, and David Lurie, eds. *The Cambridge History of Japanese Literature.* Cambridge: Cambridge University Press, 2016.

Suzuki, Sadami. *Nihon no Bungaku o Kangaeru.* Tokyo: Kadokawa Shoten, 1994.

Thunman, Noriko. *Nakahara Chūya and French Symbolism.* Stockholm: Stockholm University, Institute of Oriental Languages (Dept. of Japanese and Korean), 1983.

Chūya Nakahara, age 29 (1936). At his mother Fuku's behest, a relative who was a director at the national broadcasting network (NHK) secured him an interview with the literature department. Although he posed in this application photo looking every bit the conventional salaryman, Chūya sabotaged the endeavor by listing his work history simply as "poetry life."

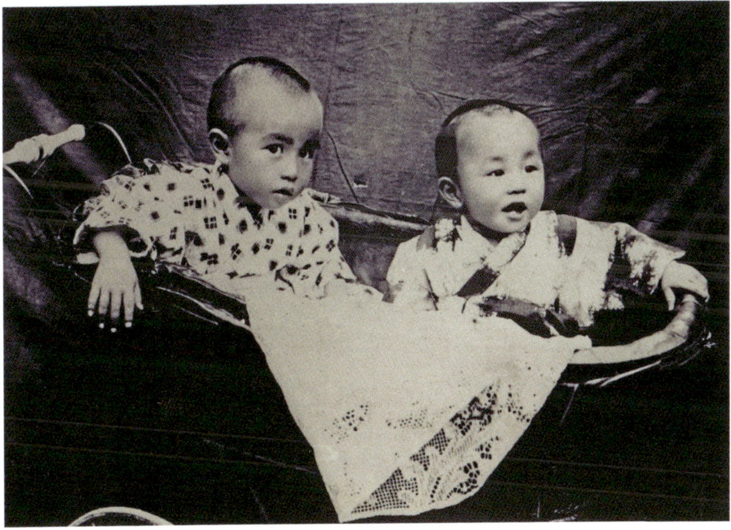

FACING PAGE, clockwise from top left: Chūya, age 1 year 4 months; Chūya with four of his five younger brothers in 1921; the Nakahara Clinic, run by his father. THIS PAGE, TOP: The Nakahara family after they moved to Kanazawa in 1912. Front row from the left: Chūya, younger brother Tsugurō, grandmother Sué and mother Fuku. Back row from the left: father Kensuke and a steward holding Kōzō. BOTTOM: With Tsugurō, who died when Chūya was eight, inspiring him to write his first poem.

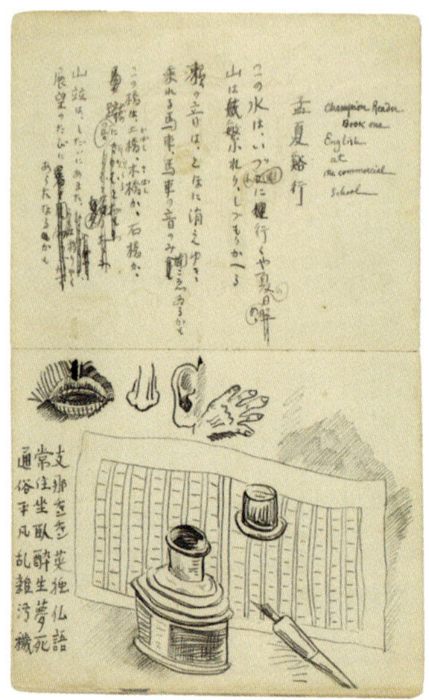

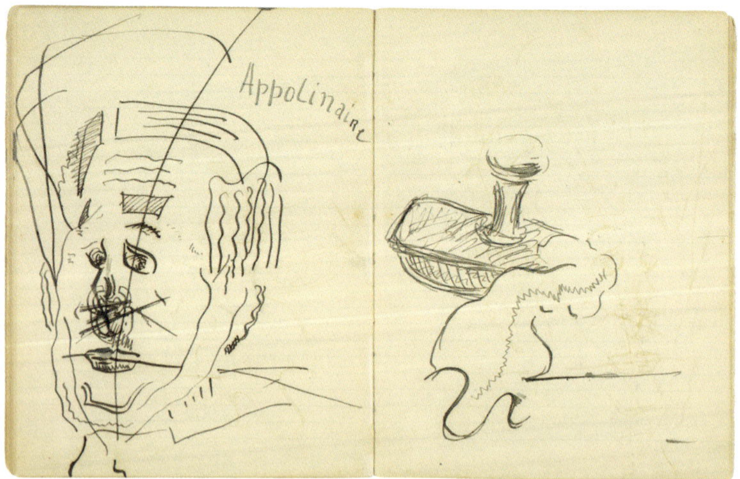

While still in elementary school, Chūya began receiving excellent marks for his calligraphy (the practice sheet at the TOP LEFT reads "Japanese cherry blossoms"; the red spirals are the teacher's mark for excellent work). He later became an occasional sketch artist in a style clearly influenced by Picasso, Matisse and other Modernist painters of Europe, peppering his journals, manuscripts and correspondence with doodles like this playful portrait of Guillaume Apollinaire.

Love Triangle: When he was only sixteen, Chūya began a relationship with Yasuko Hasegawa, a beautiful film actress three years his senior. Soon after the couple moved to Tokyo in 1925, she left him for friend and critic Hideo Kobayashi, who would become the executor of Chūya's literary estate and one of the greatest champions of his work. After Kobayashi and Yasuko eventually separated, Chūya made several unsuccessful attempts to win her back. He remained heartbroken for most of his life, and the pain haunted his poetry.

Shinkichi Takahashi (1901–1987)

Despite his short lifespan, Chūya engaged deeply in the vibrant literary scene of his day. Known for his difficult personality and wild mood swings, he still made lasting friendships and moved in circles that included many future giants of Japanese literature. *Poems of the Dadaist Shinkichi* by Shinkichi Takahashi became the first great influence on Chūya's developing aesthetic. Fellow poet Tarō Tominaga, having introduced Chūya to French Symbolist works, devastated him by committing suicide in 1925. Chūya shared his most expansive correspondence

Tarō Tominaga (1901–1925)

Yoshihiro Yasuhara (1908–1992)

with Yoshihiro Yasuhara, preserving an epistolary record of his intellectual and emotional life. Although Chūya never met Kenji Miyazawa, his pioneering use of colloquial idiom, rhythm, lexical music, and a spiritually infused vision of nature helped shape Chūya's sensibility. Close companion Shōhei Ōoka gained international fame as a war novelist and secured Chūya's legacy by writing his definitive biography. Tetsutarō Kawakami and the avant-garde Surya circle gave musical voice to many of Chūya's poems, scoring them with unconventional harmonies and rhythms.

Kenji Miyazawa (1896–1933)

Shōhei Ōoka (1909–1988)

Tetsutarō Kawakami (1902–1980)

Chūya in a wedding photo (1933) with Takako Ueno, a distant cousin six years his junior. Having failed to reconcile with Yasuko, Chūya ultimately agreed to an *omiai* (arranged marriage) set up by his mother Fuku.

Cradling his first son, Fumiya, who died just after his second birthday. A shattered Chūya remained at the boy's bedside for three days, refusing to sleep, and eventually suffered a complete breakdown. He dedicated *Songs of Bygone Days* to Fumiya's memory.

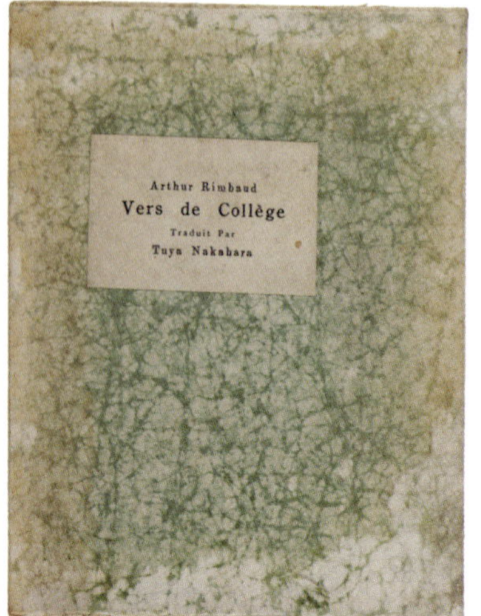

Chūya studied French relentlessly and developed into a fine translator, especially of those *poètes maudits* ("cursed poets") he admired—in particular, Rimbaud. The year before his own first collection found ink, Mikasa Shobō published his translations of Rimbaud's *Poems of School Days* [TOP LEFT; 1933] to general acclaim. There followed *Selected Poems of Rimbaud* [TOP RIGHT; Yamamoto Shoten, 1936] and *Collected Poems of Rimbaud* [BOTTOM; Noda Shoten, 1937], with a cover sketch by Verlaine.

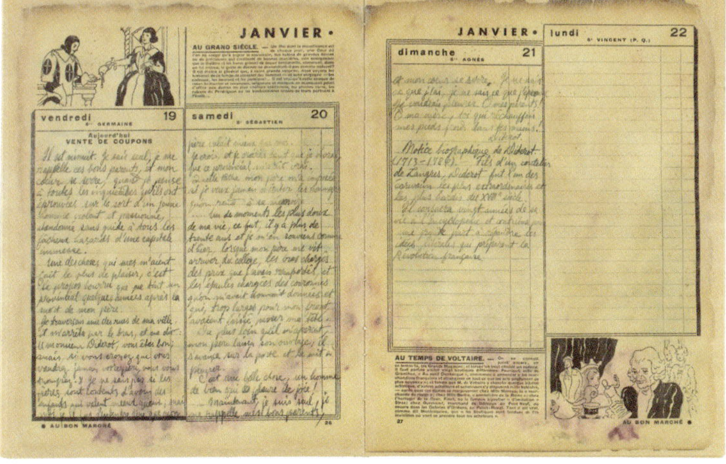

TOP: Chūya (front row, far left) in 1931 at the Tokyo School of Foreign Languages, where he studied French. It became the Tokyo University of Foreign Studies (TUFS) in 1951. BOTTOM: In his Bon Marché ("Good Value") Diary of 1937, he transcribes from the prose of writer-philosopher Denis Diderot.

First editions of the two collections Chūya compiled in his lifetime. *Goat Songs* [TOP; 1934], financed by his mother Fuku, had a print run of only 200 and sold poorly. Sogensha posthumously published 600 copies of *Songs of Bygone Days* [BOTTOM; 1938], with a reprint of 300, and it received some positive reviews. Not until after WWII, however, would the public and literary world recognize Chūya as a central voice of modern Japanese poetry.

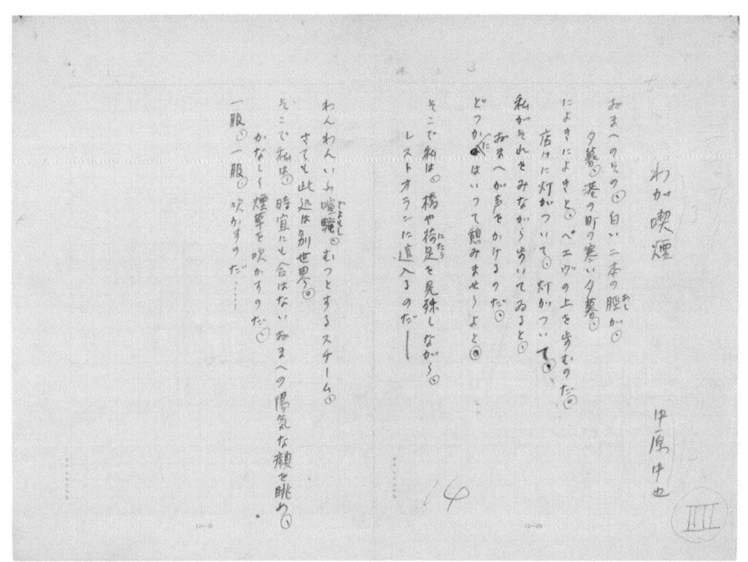

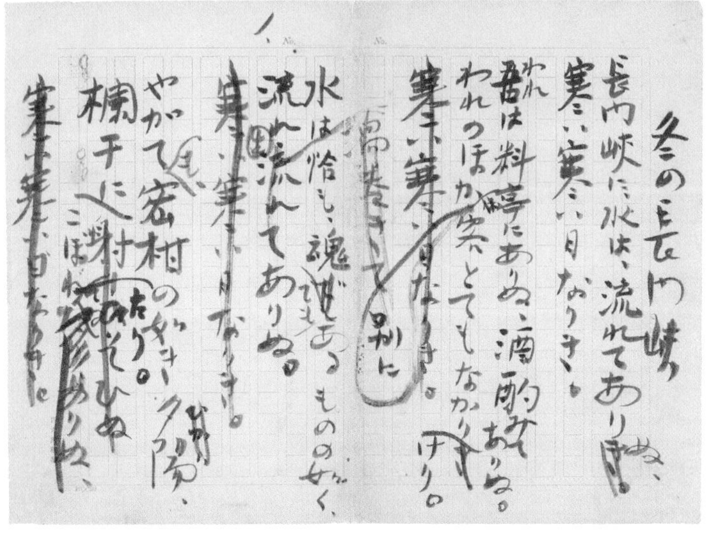

Using calligraphy brushes, ink pens and pencils, Chūya drafted his poems in an amazing variety of styles. They seemed to proliferate together with the expansion of his poetic range, as seen here in drafts of "My Smoking" [TOP] and "Chōmon Gorge in Winter" [BOTTOM].

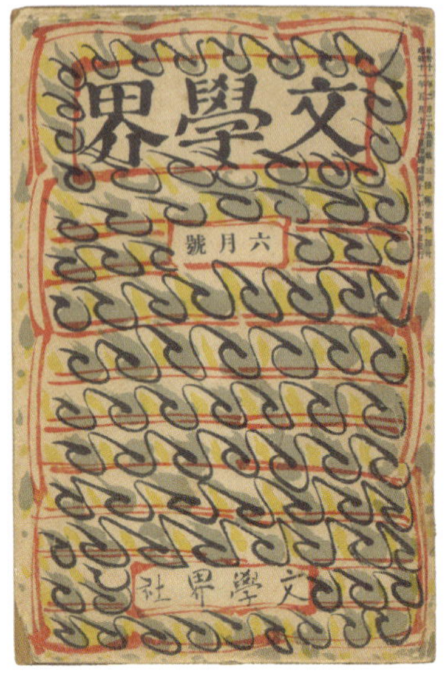

Bungakukai (Literary World)

Shiki (Four Seasons)

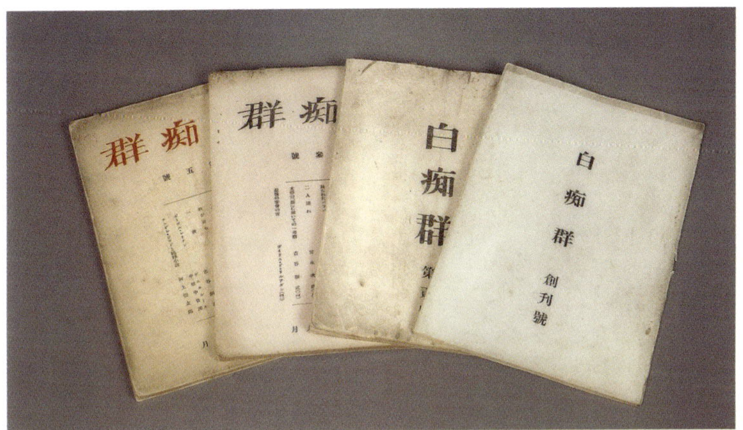

Hakuchigun (Band of Idiots)

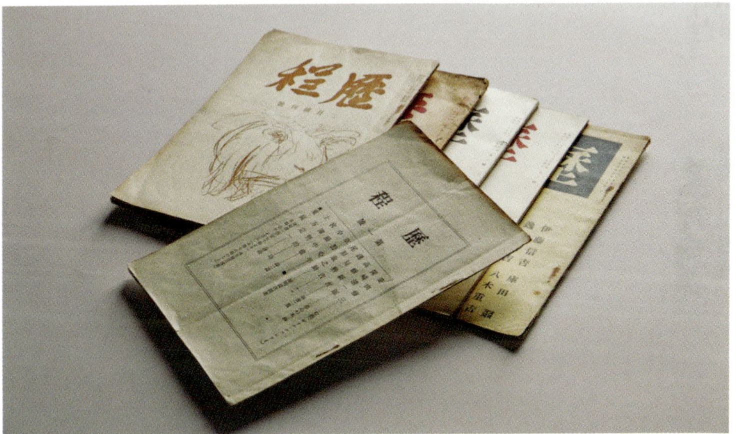

Rekitei (Trajectory)

Over the course of his brief career, Chūya contributed to an expanding range of literary and mainstream journals. Some of these were coterie magazines edited by literary friends like Hideo Kobayashi and Shimpei Kusano, which ensured him constant venues for his work. Principal among them were *Bungakukai*, *Shiki*, *Hakuchigun* (co-founded by Chūya himself) and *Rekitei*. Chūya also famously participated in their poetry readings, helping to shape Japan's early Shōwa-era literary scene. Many of his poems were adapted by the musical group Surya; the program OPPOSITE is from a 1928 performance.

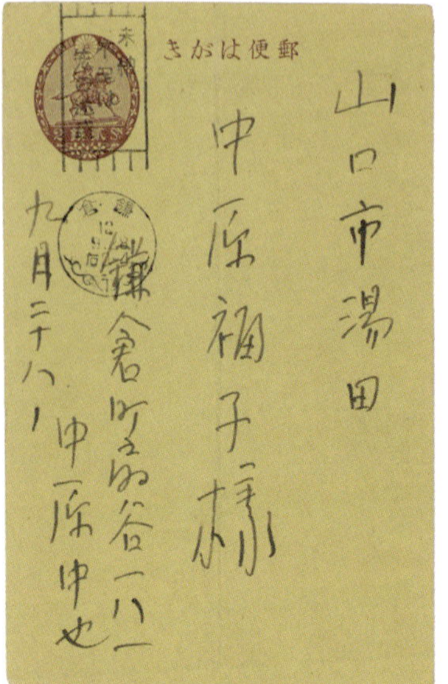

振替受取ました。坊やはすつかりよくなりましたが、まだいつもほど元気がありません、ジンウ炎はなほつてから三週間が大切ださうですから、用心してゐます。日仏学館の通信講義は、一週に二度だといふに、またはじめの答案が行つたきり帰つて来ません。はじめはこんなものかもしれませんが。
昨夜はかなりな雨でした。山のそばは故、まだ蚊がゐます。そろそろ、寒くなつて来ます。では又。僕の病気は少しはいいやうです。

TOP: Chūya sent his mother Fuku this postcard three weeks before his death. “My illness seems to be improving a little,” he wrote. BOTTOM: In 1965, Fuku and close friends Hideo Kobayashi, Hidemi Kon, Tetsutarō Kawakami, and Shōhei Ōoka attended the dedication of a memorial to Chūya’s poetry. The inscription is from the poem “Homecoming”: *this is my hometown / the wind is blowing clearly / ah what have you done with your life / the blowing wind asks me*

Acknowledgments

I wish to thank the editors of the following journals in which these poems appeared, some of them in different forms:

Adirondack Review: Hangover, Darling, Midnight Thoughts, My Smoking, One Autumn Day, Port Town Autumn, Song of Summer Going By; *AGNI:* Lost Hope; *Asymptote:* Atrophy, To Ruined Sorrow; *Boston Review:* Song of Upbringing; *Cream City Review:* The Moon, Sheep Song; *International Poetry Review:* Boyhood; *The Journal:* Dusk on a Spring Day; *Juked:* Blind Autumn; *The Kenyon Review:* Dreary Morning; *Kyoto Journal:* Autumn, Spring Night, Evening Sun; *New Orleans Review:* Summer, Tremendous Twilight; *Raritan:* Morning Song, Now is the Hour . . .; *Revolver:* Circus, Voice of Life, Winter Night Rain; *Southeast Review:* Sigh; *Subtropics:* A Fairy Tale, Song for a Summer Day; *Texas Review:* Homecoming, Deathbed.

Goat Songs
山羊の歌

EARLY POEMS

初期詩篇

Dusk on a Spring Day

tin roof snapping up senbei
in a calm spring dusk
ash thrown underhand turning pale
becomes a quiet spring dusk

ah!   is there a scarecrow?—there cannot be
will a horse neigh?—perhaps not even that
is it only to the slimy moon
that a spring dusk   is obedient?

pitter-patter the temple in the field turns red
cartwheel   in need of oil
if I speak to the historical present
they'd make a fool of me   the sky and mountains

a single roof tile   has wandered away
now the spring dusk will
without a word   move
on into its own   bloodstream

senbei: rice cracker

春の日の夕暮

トタンがセンベイ食べて
春の日の夕暮は穏かです
アンダースローされた灰が蒼ざめて
春の日の夕暮は静かです

呼！　案山子はないか——あるまい
馬 嘶くか——嘶きもしまい
ただただ月の光のヌメランとするまゝに
従順なのは　春の日の夕暮か

ポトポトと野の中に伽藍は紅く
荷馬車の車輪　油を失ひ
私が歴史的現在に物を云へば
嘲る嘲る　空と山とが

瓦が一枚　はぐれました
これから春の日の夕暮は
無言ながら　前進します
自らの　静脈管の中へです

The Moon

More solitary than ever tonight, the moon
wonders at her doubting foster father.
Time washes a silver tide into the desert.
An old man's earlobes glow like fireflies.

Ah, forgotten embankments of canals,
tanks, the earth resounding in my chest.
The moon takes a cigarette
from a rusty case and smokes lazily.

Heels over head, seven celestial nymphs
keep dancing around about,
but give no comfort

to the moon's heart, weltering in disgrace.
O far-flung stars!
The moon awaits her executioner.

月

今宵月はいよよ愁しく、
養父の疑惑に瞳を瞬る。
秒刻は銀波を砂漠に流し
老男の耳朶は蛍光をともす。

あゝ忘られた運河の岸堤
胸に残つた戦車の地音
銹びつく鑵の煙草とりいで
月は懶く喫つてゐる。

それのめぐりを七人の天女は
趾頭舞踊しつづけてゐるが、
汚辱に浸る月の心に

なんの慰愛もあたへはしない。
遠にちらばる星と星よ！
おまへの創手を月は待つてる

Circus

for a number of eras
    there was a brown war

for a number of eras
    a gale blew in winter

for a number of eras
    here tonight a drinking party
        here tonight a drinking party

there is a high beam in the circus tent
    just one trapeze
an invisible trapeze

head down and arms dangling
    under dirty cotton of the big top
see saw see and saw

close to which white light
    breathes out a cheap ribbon

the audience are a bunch of sardines
    throats gurgle like oyster shells
see saw see and saw

        outside is dark dark on dark
        night waning forever
        with nostalgia for the damned parachutes
        see saw see and saw

サーカス

幾時代かがありまして
　茶色い戦争ありました

幾時代かがありまして
　冬は疾風吹きました

幾時代かがありまして
　今夜此処での一と殷盛り
　　今夜此処での一と殷盛り

サーカス小屋は高い梁
　そこに一つのブランコだ
見えるともないブランコだ

頭倒さに手を垂れて
　汚れ木綿の屋蓋のもと
ゆあーん　ゆよーん　ゆやゆよん

それの近くの白い灯が
　安値いリボンと息を吐き

観客様はみな鰯
　咽喉が鳴ります牡蠣殻と
ゆあーん　ゆよーん　ゆやゆよん

　　屋外は真ッ闇　闇の闇
　　夜は刧々と更けまする
　　落下傘奴のノスタルヂアと
　　ゆあーん　ゆよーん　ゆやゆよん

Spring Night

Dull silver, the window gently frames
  a branch of flowers. Peach flowers.

Moonlight faints into the garden's
  topsoil . . . velvet beauty spots.

Ah, nothing, there's nothing to it:
  trees, be bashful as you come and go.

This remote sound offers
  no hope, nor shrift.

Only pious mountain builders,
  along with the dream caravan's steps, are faintly seen.

Barely visible through the glass,
  a silk robe the color of sand.

From the breast, piano music is ringing out—
  no forebears or parents.

Ah, where did I bury my dog?
  Saffron yellow this surge,
    this spring night.

春の夜

燻銀なる窓枠の中になごやかに
　一枝の花、桃色の花。

月光うけて失神し
　庭の土面は附黒子。

あゝこともなしこともなし
　樹々よはにかみ立ちまはれ。

このすゞろなる物の音に
　希望はあらず、さてはまた、
　　懺悔もあらず。

山虔しき木工のみ、
　夢の裡なる隊商のその足竝もほのみゆれ。

窓の中にはさはやかの、おぼろかの
　砂の色せる絹衣。

かびろき胸のピアノ鳴り
　祖先はあらず、親も消ぬ。

埋みし犬の何処にか、
　蕃紅花色に湧きいづる
　　春の夜や。

Morning Song

the ceiling   fades to scarlet
   sunlight reaching through   a gap in the shutters
shades of a rustic   military band
   my hands find   nothing to do

birdsongs   are inaudible
   and the sky appears   pale blue today
crestfallen   one's heart
   without anything   to admonish it

scent of pine resin   troubles me at dawn
   so many dreams   I lost
ah forests   murmur in the wind

calm sky   goes on forever
   ah fading away   down the riverbank
so many   beautiful dreams

朝の歌

天井に　朱きいろいで
　戸の隙を　洩れ入る光、
鄙びたる　軍楽の憶ひ
　手にてなす　なにごともなし。

小鳥らの　うたはきこえず
　空は今日　はなだ色らし、
倦んじてし　人のこころを
　諫めする　なにものもなし。

樹脂の香に　朝は悩まし
　うしなひし　さまざまのゆめ、
森竝は　風に鳴るかな

ひろごりて　たひらかの空、
　土手づたひ　きえてゆくかな
うつくしき　さまざまの夢。

Deathbed

dull gray autumn sky
gleam in the eye of a black horse
   dry lily fallen
   ah   my vacant heart

no God with guiding hands
a woman died by the window
   white sky turns a blind eye
   white wind blows coldly

beside the window
she washed her hair with gentle hands
   morning sun flowing away
   the sound of dripping water

town after lively town
a tangle of children's voices
   yet   what will happen to this soul?
   will it disperse   become the sky?

臨終

秋空は鈍色にして
黒馬の瞳のひかり
　水涸れて落つる百合花
　あゝ　こころうつろなるかな

神もなくしるべもなくて
窓近く婦の逝きぬ
　白き空盲ひてありて
　白き風冷たくありぬ

窓際に髪を洗へば
その腕の優しくありぬ
　朝の日は澪れてありぬ
　水の音したたりてゐぬ

町々はさやぎてありぬ
子等の声もつれてありぬ
　しかはあれ　この魂はいかにとなるか？
　うすらぎて　空となるか？

Urban Summer Night

Moon in the sky like a medal,
building at the street-corner like an organ,
and worn out revelers go home singing.
—*Hey, your high collar's crooked—*

Lips hanging open,
they look somehow sad at heart.
Their heads become dark clods of earth
and they just go by singing, *laa-laa.*

Business and ancestors—
although these they don't forget,
the urban summer night wanes—

Deepening to dead gunpowder
as streetlight soaks into their eyes,
they just go by singing, *laa-laa.*

都会の夏の夜

月は空にメダルのやうに、
街角に建物はオルガンのやうに、
遊び疲れた男どち唱ひながらに帰つてゆく。
——イカムネ・カラアがまがつてゐる——

その唇は肱ききつて
その心は何か悲しい。
頭が暗い土塊になつて、
ただもうラアラア唱つてゆくのだ。

商用のことや祖先のことや
忘れてゐるといふではないが、
都会の夏の夜の更——

死んだ火薬と深くして
眼に外燈の滲みいれば
ただもうラアラア唱つてゆくのだ。

One Autumn Day

This morning, people late to rise are
drowned by sounds of wind against doors, of wheels,
in the ocean where the Sirens live.

No more talk in summer night stalls,
nor conscience of the carpenter.
All is ancient history
and the horizon's eye color beyond the granite.

Today everything is obedient under the consular office flag,
and I know nothing besides a tin, the plaza, and drums
  of heaven.
Without a care for the husky voices of mollusks,
in the park, making a squat purple shadow,
  an infant puts sand in its mouth.

  (A pale blue platform,
  noisy girls and scornful Yanks,
  I hate them, hate them!)

Hands thrust in pockets,
down the alley and out to the wharf,
I'm going in search of something
like rags to suit my soul for the day.

秋の一日

こんな朝、遅く目覚める人達は
戸にあたる風と轍との音によつて、
サイレンの棲む海に溺れる。

夏の夜の露店の会話と、
建築家の良心はもうない。
あらゆるものは古代歴史と
花崗岩のかなたの地平の目の色。

今朝はすべてが領事館旗のもとに従順で、
私は錫と広場と天鼓のほかのなんにも知らない。
軟体動物のしやがれ声にも気をとめないで、
紫の蹲んだ影して公園で、
　乳児は口に砂を入れる。

　　(水色のプラットホームと
　　躁ぐ少女と嘲笑ふヤンキイは
　　いやだ　いやだ！)

ぽけっとに手を突込んで
路次を抜け、波止場に出でて
今日の日の魂に合ふ
布切屑をでも探して来よう。

Twilight

On the surface of a dull, quiet pond,
lotus leaves gather and wave.
Since they have thick skins,
The leaves make only a rustling sound.

When they make that sound, my heart wavers,
eyes follow a dim horizon . . .
I see only the blackest mountains.
—Lost things never return.

Nothing could be sadder than this sorrow.
A smell of grass roots quietly finds me.
I'm being watched by stones in field earth.

—Made up my mind at last: I won't farm it!
Standing in twilight, idle and still,
when the image of my father starts to bother me, I just
take a step or two.

黄昏

渋つた仄暗い池の面で、
寄り合つた蓮の葉が揺れる。
蓮の葉は、図太いので
こそこそとしか音をたてない。

音をたてると私の心が揺れる、
目が薄明るい地平線を逐ふ……
黒々と山がのぞきかかるばつかりだ
——失はれたものはかへつて来ない。

なにが悲しいつたつてこれほど悲しいことはない
草の根の匂ひが静かに鼻にくる、
畑の土が石といつしよに私を見てゐる。

——竟に私は耕やさうとは思はない！
じいつと茫然 黄昏の中に立つて、
なんだか父親の映像が気になりだすと一歩二歩
　歩みだすばかりです

Midnight Thoughts

This is bubbling calcium's
sudden
dehydration—an innocent girl's cry,
a bag shop wife's evening snot.

The grove twilight is
a cracked mother.
Insects buzz around the treetops,
their funny pacifier dance.

Hunting dog of waving hair unseen,
hunter takes his humpback away.
The field near the forest
becomes a hill!

Margaret approaches the black shore,
veil ruffled by the wind.
Her body must plunge into
the hard God's father ocean!

Standing on the cliff above her,
a genie draws an odd stripe.
Her memory: the clean-up of a sad study.
She must die before long.

深夜の思ひ

これは泡立つカルシウムの
乾きゆく
急速な——頑ぜない女の児の泣声だ、
鞄屋の女房の夕の鼻汁だ。

林の黄昏は
擦れた母親。
虫の飛交ふ梢のあたり、
舐子のお道化た踊り。

波うつ毛の猟犬見えなく、
猟師は猫背を向ふに運ぶ。
森を控へた草地が
坂になる！

黒き浜辺にマルガレエテが歩み寄する
ヴェールを風に千々にされながら。
彼女の肉は跳び込まねばならぬ、
厳しき神の父なる海に！

崖の上の彼女の上に
精霊が怪しげなる條を描く。
彼女の思ひ出は悲しい書斎の取片附け
彼女は直きに死なねばならぬ。

Winter Night Rain

Throughout the black winter night
it rained heavily.
—Awful withered daikon thrown out in the twilight,
that's how horrible things had been—
and now it rains heavily
throughout the black winter night.
I even hear the voices of girls who have died,
aé, ao, aé, ao, éo, aéo, éo!
Floating around in that rain,
they melted without notice, those milky ice packs . . .
And now throughout the black
winter night it rains heavily,
and my mother's obi cord
is also swept away by rainwater, crushed,
and all those human mercies,
were they only tangerine-colored in the end? . . .

daikon: giant radish with a mild flavor; a staple of Japanese cooking

obi: kimono belt; generally tied with a colorful braided cord (*obijime*) to keep it from loosening

冬の雨の夜

冬の黒い夜をこめて
どしやぶりの雨が降つてゐた。
——夕明下に投げいだされた、萎れ大根の陰惨
　さ、
あれはまだしも結構だつた——
今や黒い冬の夜をこめ
どしやぶりの雨が降つてゐる。
亡き乙女達の声さへがして
aé, ao, aé, ao, éo, aéo, éo!
その雨の中を漂ひながら
いつだか消えてなくなつた、あの乳白の
　脬囊たち……
今や黒い冬の夜をこめ
どしやぶりの雨が降つてゐて、
わが母上の帯締めも
雨水に流れ、潰れてしまひ、
人の情けのかずかずも
竟に蜜柑の色のみだつた？……

Homecoming

pillars are dry and so is the garden
today is a beautiful day
    under the porch a spider's web
    helplessly wavering

in the mountains even dead trees sigh
ah what a beautiful day
    by the roadside shadows of grass
    show innocent grief

this is my hometown
the wind is blowing clearly
    cry without shame
    I even hear an old woman's low voice

ah   what have you done with your life
the blowing wind asks me

帰郷

柱も庭も乾いてゐる
今日は好い天気だ
　　縁の下では蜘蛛の巣が
　　心細さうに揺れてゐる

山では枯木も息を吐く
あゝ今日は好い天気だ
　　路傍の草影が
　　あどけない愁みをする

これが私の故里だ
さやかに風も吹いてゐる
　　心置なく泣かれよと
　　年増婦の低い声もする

あゝ　おまへはなにをして来たのだと……
吹き来る風が私に云ふ

Tremendous Twilight

Constant wind wearying me, but then
grasses ripple and I see
the Hayato people of yore.

Silver bamboo spears extend
along a shore.
—Relying on the hearts of minnows.

Indifferently, the wind blows.
Bodies spread across the earth—
The sky stands on a dais.

House after house, wise liegemen
hiding nicotine-stained teeth.

凄じき黄昏

捲き起る、風も物憂き頃ながら、
草は靡きぬ、我はみぬ、
遐き昔の隼人等を。

銀紙色の竹槍の、
汀に沿ひて、つづきけり。
——雑魚の心を俟みつつ。

吹く風誘はず、地の上の
敷きある屍——
空、演壇に立ちあがる。

家々は、賢き陪臣、
ニコチンに、汚れたる歯を押匿す。

Song of Summer Going By

The treetops took a deep breath,
and the sky high, high above was looking at them.
A pilgrim came along in a hurry to find
glass that had fallen on the radiant sand.

The mountain's verge becomes clear, clear,
and purifies the mouths of goldfish and girl.
On that plane flying this way
I put some insect tears yesterday.

The wind sends a ribbon into the sky,
and I think I shall talk of the once-fallen sea
and about its waves.

I shall talk of cavalry, the motion of upper limbs,
a petty official's red shoes,
and a bicycle that goes along the mountain
without a rider.

逝く夏の歌

並木の梢が深く息を吸つて、
空は高く高く、それを見てゐた。
日の照る砂地に落ちてゐた硝子を、
歩み来た旅人は周章てて見付けた。

山の端は、澄んで澄んで、
金魚や娘の口の中を清くする。
飛んでくるあの飛行機には、
昨日私が昆虫の涙を塗つておいた。

風はリボンを空に送り、
私は嘗て陥落した海のことを
その浪のことを語らうと思ふ。

騎兵連隊や上肢の運動や、
下級官吏の赤靴のことや、
山沿ひの道を乗手もなく行く
自転車のことを語らうと思ふ。

Dreary Morning

The sound of a shallow stream comes to the mountain.
Spring light is a stone.
Water pours from the kakei
like an old woman reading a story.

Sang, with my isinglass mouth.
Sang, falling backwards.
Dry and hoarse, my heart
walked the tightrope between rocks.

A mysterious fire blazes into the sky!

A deluge of noise crowns me!

. . . .

Absently, I clap my hands . . .

kakei: a bamboo or wooden gutter that guides water, often into a stone basin or pond. Typically found in traditional Japanese gardens, it is constructed so that the meditative sound of trickling water—and with some, the rhythmic knock of the spout against the basin—can be heard.

悲しき朝

河瀬の音が山に来る、
春の光は、石のやうだ。
筧の水は、物語る
白髪の嫗にさも肖てる。

雲母の口して歌つたよ、
背ろに倒れ、歌つたよ、
心は涸れて皺枯れて、
巌の上の、綱渡り、

知れざる炎、空にゆき！

響の雨は、濡れ冠る！

・・・・・・・・・・・・・・・・・

われかにかくに手を拍く……

Song for a Summer Day

Motionless blue sky.
Not so much as a wisp of cloud.
  The summer noonday quiet
  makes even tar gleam with clear light.

There's something about the summer sky,
something that arouses pity.
  Burnt and brazen sunflowers
  are in bloom around the country station.

Like a mother skillfully raising her children,
a train blows its whistle.
  When it passes by the mountain.

Passing by the mountain,
a train blows its whistle like a mother
  in the summer noonday heat.

夏の日の歌

青い空は動かない、
雲片一つあるでない。
　　夏の真昼の静かには
　　タールの光も清くなる。

夏の空には何かがある、
いぢらしく思はせる何かがある、
　　焦げて図太い向日葵が
　　田舎の駅には咲いてゐる。

上手に子供を育てゆく、
母親に似て汽車の汽笛は鳴る。
　　山の近くを走る時。

山の近くを走りながら、
母親に似て汽車の汽笛は鳴る。
　　夏の真昼の暑い時。

Evening Sun

Hills put hands on their hearts
and are chased away.
The sunset is a tender,
golden color.

Field grasses sing
a folk song,
and mountain trees
age, acquire thrifty natures.

At the moment I was there,
a little boy stepped
on the meat of a shellfish.

Just then, a tough man's
modest resignation went
off with folded arms.

夕照

丘々は、胸に手を当て
退けり。
落陽は、慈愛の色の
金のいろ。

原に草、
鄙唄うたひ
山に樹々、
老いてつましき心ばせ。

かゝる折しも我ありぬ
小児に踏まれし
貝の肉。

かゝるをりしも剛直の、
さあれゆかしきあきらめよ
腕拱みながら歩み去る。

Port Town Autumn

Morning sun shines on a stone cliff
and the autumn sky is perfectly beautiful.
The port visible over there,
couldn't it also be the horns of a snail?

In town, some people clean their pipes.
A tile roof stretches out,
the sky breaks.
An officers' holiday—they wear dotera.

"When I am born again . . . "
sings a sailor.
"Let's jump on the whee-ee-ee—ka-*boom!* . . . "
sings a wily old woman.

> A port town autumn day
> is gentle madness.
> I, on that day in my life,
> lost a chair.

dotera: a quilted housecoat worn over a kimono

港市の秋

石崖に、朝陽が射して
秋空は美しいかぎり。
むかふに見える港は、
蝸牛の角でもあるのか

町では人々煙管の掃除。
甍は伸びをし
空は割れる。
役人の休み日——どてら姿だ。

『今度生れたら……』
海員が唄ふ。
『ぎーこたん、ばつたりしよ……』
狸婆々がうたふ。

　　港の市の秋の日は、
　　大人しい発狂。
　　私はその日人生に、
　　椅子を失くした。

Sigh

for Tetsutarō Kawakami

A sigh will go out to a bog at night
and blink within the miasma.
The blink will continue grudgingly and make a
snapping sound.
Trees will resemble the napes of young scholar
colleagues' necks.

When dawn breaks, a window will open onto the horizon.
A cart-drawing peasant will leave for the city.
The sigh will become deeper still,
like the cart sound echoing through the hills.

A pine tree pushing into a field from a mountain's verge
will keep an eye on me.
It will look like an ordinary uncle who never laughs.
As if God were catching fish from the depths of an air
stratum.

When the sky becomes overcast, locust eyes will peep
through sandy earth.
A distant town will look like lime.
Peter the Great's eyeballs glimmer in the clouds.

ためいき

河上徹太郎に

ためいきは夜の沼にゆき、
瘴気の中で瞬きをするであらう。
その瞬きは怨めしさうにながれながら、
　パチンと音を立てるだらう。
木々が若い学者仲間の、
　頸すぢのやうであるだらう。

夜が明けたら地平線に、窓が開くだらう。
荷車を挽いた百姓が、町の方へ行くだらう。
ためいきはなほ深くして、
丘に響きあたる荷車の音のやうであるだらう。

野原に突出た山ノ端の松が、
　私を看守つてゐるだらう。
それはあつさりしてても笑はない、
　叔父さんのやうであるだらう。
神様が気層の底の、魚を捕つてゐるやうだ。

空が曇つたら、蝗螽の瞳が、
　砂土の中に覗くだらう。
遠くに町が、石灰みたいだ。
ピョートル大帝の目玉が、雲の中で光つてゐる。

Spring Memory

milk vetches that I had plucked
   when it was time to go home for dinner
with spring mist rising in the air
      I flung them on the ground

one last sorry glance
   then casually wiped my hands
and ran off down the road
      (the sky in twilight!)

I entered my house to find it
   mingling comfortably
an autumn hill at dusk or furnace smoke
      something that made me feel dizzy

      a luxurious old mansion's
            quadrille   waving skirts
            quadrille   waving skirts
      dying away in time   quadrille!

春の思ひ出

摘み溜めしれんげの華を
　夕餉に帰る時刻となれば
立迷ふ春の暮靄の
　　土の上に叩きつけ

いまひとたびは未練で眺め
　さりげなく手を拍きつつ
路の上を走りてくれば
　　（暮れのこる空よ！）

わが家へと入りてみれば
　なごやかにうちまじりつつ
秋の日の夕陽の丘か炊煙か
　　われを暈めかすもののあり

　　古き代の富みし館の
　　　　カドリール　ゆらゆるスカーツ
　　　　カドリール　ゆらゆるスカーツ
　　何時の日か絶えんとはする　カドリール！

Autumn Night Sky

My, what a festive sight!
Each speaks after her own fashion, and yet
all maintain a touch of elegance,
all are ladies.
    While the lower world is an autumn night,
the upper world is bustling.

Golden lanterns shine
on a polished floor.
Small heads, long trains,
and not a single chair.
    While the lower world is an autumn night,
the upper world is aglow.

The faintly bright upper world—
a shadow festival from the old days,
calm, gentle commotion,
an evening banquet.
    Yet, even as I was watching from the lower world,
it disappeared without my noticing.

秋の夜空

これはまあ、おにぎはしい、
みんなてんでなことをいふ
それでもつれぬみやびさよ
いづれ揃つて夫人たち。
　　下界は秋の夜といふに
上天界のにぎはしさ。

すべすべしてゐる床の上、
金のカンテラ点いてゐる。
小さな頭、長い裳裾、
椅子は一つもないのです。
　　下界は秋の夜といふに
上天界のあかるさよ。

ほんのりあかるい上天界
遐き昔の影祭、
しづかなしづかな賑はしさ
上天界の夜の宴。
　　私は下界で見てゐたが、
知らないあひだに退散した。

Hangover

Morning, the dull sun shining
  and it's windy.
A thousand angels
  play basketball.

I close my eyes:
  it's a sad drunkenness.
A derelict kerosene
  heater rusts in white.

Morning, the dull sun shining,
  and it's windy.
A thousand angels
  play basketball.

宿酔

朝、鈍い日が照つてて
　風がある。
千の天使が
　バスケットボールする。

私は目をつむる、
　かなしい酔ひだ。
もう不用になつたストーヴが、
　白つぽく銹びてゐる。

朝、鈍い日が照つてて
　風がある。
千の天使が
　バスケットボールする。

BOYHOOD

少年時

Boyhood

A summer day beat down on purple stones,
the garden surface lazing in vermilion.

Vapors rose against the far horizon
as if to signify the end of the world.

The low, wind-buffeted wheat fields
looked hazy and gray.

Like the shadow made by a flying cloud,
the age-old figure of a titan bestrode them—

Early one summer afternoon,
at an hour when people take naps,
I ran through a field . . .

Biting hope in my lip,
eyes glossy, I surrendered . . .
O, alive, I was alive!

少年時

　黝い石に夏の日が照りつけ、
庭の地面が、朱色に睡つてゐた。

地平の果に蒸気が立つて、
世の亡ぶ、兆のやうだつた。

麦田には風が低く打ち、
おぼろで、灰色だつた。

翔びゆく雲の落とす影のやうに、
田の面を過ぎる、昔の巨人の姿——

夏の日の午過ぎ時刻
誰彼の午睡するとき、
私は野原を走つて行つた……

私は希望を唇に噛みつぶして
私はギロギロする目で諦めてゐた……
噫、生きてゐた、私は生きてゐた！

Blind Autumn

I

Wind picks up and waves are rumbling
  as I raise my arms before infinity.

Coming into view now, small red flowers,
  but eventually they too will be crushed.

Wind picks up and waves are rumbling
  as I raise my arms before infinity.

How often have I sighed despairingly
  at the thought that I would never return . . .

My youth is already a hardened artery
  through which flow red spider lilies and evening sun.

Quiet, gorgeous and brimming,
  like the last smile of a leaving woman,

solemn, rich, desolate,
  unusual, warm, glittery, it touches my heart . . .
    Ah, how it touches my heart . . .

Wind picks up and waves are rumbling
  as I raise my arms before infinity.

盲目の秋

I

風が立ち、浪が騒ぎ、
　無限の前に腕を振る。

その間、小さな紅の花が見えはするが、
　それもやがては潰れてしまふ。

風が立ち、浪が騒ぎ、
　無限のまへに腕を振る。

もう永遠に帰らないことを思つて
　酷白な嘆息するのも幾たびであらう……

私の青春はもはや堅い血管となり、
　その中を曼珠沙華と夕陽とがゆきすぎる。

それはしづかで、きらびやかで、なみなみと湛へ、
　去りゆく女が最後にくれる笑ひのやうに、

厳かで、ゆたかで、それでゐて佗しく
　異様で、温かで、きらめいて胸に残る……
　　あゝ、胸に残る……

風が立ち、浪が騒ぎ、
　無限のまへに腕を振る。

II

How this may change, how that may change,
I don't care.

What this means, what that means,
these really don't matter.

All you need is faith in yourself!
Leave everything else as it is . . .

Faith, faith, faith, faith—
the only thing that doesn't make your deeds sinful.

Just be at your ease, cheerful, and as quietly as a wisp
of straw,
fill the kettle with morning dew and spring to your feet!

II

これがどうならうと、あれがどうならうと、
そんなことはどうでもいいのだ。

これがどういふことであらうと、それがどういふ
　ことであらうと、
そんなことはなほさらどうだつていいのだ。

人には自恃があればよい！
その余はすべてなるまゝだ……

自恃だ、自恃だ、自恃だ、自恃だ、
ただそれだけが人の行ひを罪としない。

平気で、陽気で、藁束のやうにしむみりと、
朝霧を煮釜に填めて、跳起きられればよい！

III

My Santa Maria!
   I *did* cough up blood!
And since you didn't want my sympathy,
   I was well and truly beaten . . .

Although that's because I showed no deference,
   although that's because I had no guts,
since it was so natural to love you,
   you loved me too, but . . .

Ah! My Santa Maria!
   Though there's no helping it now,
I'll tell you something—

that you can love a person naturally, but naturally
   doesn't happen so often,
and that's something not just anyone's allowed to know.

III

私の聖母！
　とにかく私は血を吐いた！　……
おまへが情けをうけてくれないので、
　とにかく私はまゐつてしまつた……

それといふのも私が素直でなかつたからでもあるが、
　それといふのも私に意気地がなかつたからでもあるが、
私がおまへを愛することがごく自然だつたので、
　おまへもわたしを愛してゐたのだが……

おゝ！　私の聖母！
　いまさらどうしやうもないことではあるが、
せめてこれだけ知るがいい——

ごく自然に、だが自然に愛せるといふことは、
　そんなにたびたびあることでなく、
そしてこのことを知ることが、さう誰にでも許されてはゐないのだ。

IV

Would she at least open her heart to me
when I'm dying?
For that, don't put on powder.
For that, don't put on powder.

Just silently open your heart
and radiate toward my eyes.
Please don't think of anything,
anything to do with me.

Just let your eyes well up,
breathe warmly.
If the tears flow,

you could fall on me suddenly
to take my life.
Then I would comfortably follow a snaky path up to the land of the dead.

IV

せめて死の時には、
あの女が私の上に胸を披いてくれるでせうか。
　その時は白粧をつけてゐてはいや、
　その時は白粧をつけてゐてはいや。

ただ静かにその胸を披いて、
私の眼に輻射してゐて下さい。
　何にも考へてくれてはいや、
　たとへ私のために考へてくれるのでもいや。

ただはららかにはららかに涙を含み、
あたたかく息づいてゐて下さい。
——もしも涙がながれてきたら、

いきなり私の上にうつ俯して、
それで私を殺してしまつてもいい。
すれば私は心地よく、うねうねの暝土の径を昇
　りゆく。

My Smoking

Your two white legs
 at dusk, the chilly dusk of a port town,
wind happily along the pavement.
 Stores have their lights on, they're lit up,
and I walk by looking at them,
 hear you say to me,
"Let's stop somewhere and have a rest."

Then I, leaving bridges and cargo boats behind,
 enter the restaurant—
roars and clamor, thickening steam,
 such a different world.
Then I, gazing ineptly at your happy face,
 sadly smoke my cigarette.
Puff, puff, I smoke it . . .

わが喫煙

おまへのその、白い二本の脛が、
　夕暮、港の町の寒い夕暮、
によきによきと、ペエヴの上を歩むのだ。
　店々に灯がついて、灯がついて、
私がそれをみながら歩いてゐると、
　おまへが声をかけるのだ、
どつかにはひつて憩みませうよと。

そこで私は、橋や荷足を見残しながら、
　レストオランに這入るのだ——
わんわんいふ喧騒、むつとするスチーム、
　さても此処は別世界。
そこで私は、時宜にも合はないおまへの陽気な
　顔を眺め、
　かなしく煙草を吹かすのだ、
一服、一服、吹かすのだ……

Darling

At night a beautiful soul cries
    —*that* girl is the one, but—
at night a beautiful soul cries,
    saying "I may as well die . . . "

Across the damp field's black earth, short grass,
    the night wind is blowing,
and "I may as well die, I may as well die,"
    says the beautiful soul.

At night, the sky high above, wind blowing delicately,
    there was nothing I could do but pray . . .

妹よ

夜、うつくしい魂は涕いて、
　——かの女こそ正当なのに——
夜、うつくしい魂は涕いて、
　もう死んだつていいよう……といふのであつた。

湿つた野原の黒い土、短い草の上を
　夜風は吹いて、
死んだつていいよう、死んだつていいよう、と、
　うつくしい魂は涕くのであつた。

夜、み空はたかく、吹く風はこまやかに
　——祈るよりほか、わたくしに、すべはなか
　　　つた……

Self-Portrait on a Cold Night

Although not so luminous,
I hang onto the reins
to make it through this gloomy place!
If my will is clear
I will not sigh over the winter night,
the misfortune of people's impatience,
the hum of girls led around by desire,
but feel them as trivial punishments
and let them prick my skin.

Staggering along in silence,
with almost a sense of ritual
I protest my own idleness
going under the winter moon.

To be cheerful, frank, and not sell out
is what my soul desired!

寒い夜の自我像

きらびやかでもないけれど
この一本の手綱をはなさず
この陰暗の地域を過ぎる！
その志明らかなれば
冬の夜を我は嘆かず
人々の憔懆のみの愁しみや
憧れに引廻される女等の鼻唄を
わが瑣細なる罪と感じ
そが、わが皮膚を刺すにまかす。

蹌踉めくままに静もりを保ち、
聊かは儀文めいた心地をもつて
われはわが怠惰を諫める
寒月の下を往きながら。

陽気で、坦々として、而も己を売らないことをと、
わが魂の願ふことであつた！

Tree Shade

the shrine gate basks in sunlight
and elm leaves gently sway
a summer noon's lush tree shade
quiets my regret

gloomy regret   forever hounding me
my past was full of stupid broken laughter
that turned to tearful darkness
a persistent fatigue

thus now from morning to night
I have no life other than submission
yet without a grudge and in an absent way
my eyes look up at the sky……

the shrine gate basks in sunlight
and elm leaves gently sway
a summer noon's lush tree shade
quiets my regret

木蔭

神社の鳥居が光をうけて
楡の葉が小さく揺すれる
夏の昼の青々した木蔭は
私の後悔を宥めてくれる

暗い後悔　いつでも附纏ふ後悔
馬鹿々々しい破笑にみちた私の過去は
やがて涙つぽい晦暝となり
やがて根強い疲労となつた

かくて今では朝から夜まで
忍従することのほかに生活を持たない
怨みもなく喪心したやうに
空を見上げる私の眼……

神社の鳥居が光をうけて
楡の葉が小さく揺すれる
夏の昼の青々した木蔭は
私の後悔を宥めてくれる

Lost Hope

Gone to the dark sky,
  hope that was afire in my youth.

Still, like a summer night star,
  it appears and fades, still now.

Gone to the dark sky
  my dreams, the hope of my youth,

and now I hang my head
  and make myself grim, like a beast.

I have no way of knowing
  when this misery will end.

It's like seeing the moon
  from an ocean where I'm drowning.

The waters are so deep,
  the moon so clear—

poor hope that burned in my youth
  has already vanished in the dark sky.

失せし希望

暗き空へと消え行きぬ
　わが若き日を燃えし希望は。

夏の夜の星の如くは今もなほ
　遐きみ空に見え隠る、今もなほ。

暗き空へと消えゆきぬ
　わが若き日の夢は希望は。

今はた此処に打伏して
　獣の如くは、暗き思ひす。

そが暗き思ひいつの日
　晴れんとの知るよしなくて、

溺れたる夜の海より
　空の月、望むが如し。

その浪はあまりに深く
　その月はあまりに清く、

あはれわが若き日を燃えし希望の
　今ははや暗き空へと消え行きぬ。

Summer

fatigue   ennui   how it feels to cough up blood
again today sun shines on fields   on wheat
sorrow   how it feels to drip   away in the sky
fatigue   ennui   how it feels to cough up blood

the sky burns   the fields extend
clouds float   dazzling light
again today the sun glows   the earth drips
with aching over how it feels to cough up blood

the heart's history like a storm
as though it had come to an end
as though there were no clue that could be followed
  from there
drips beyond the burning sun

I am left   as a corpse—
with aching sorrow over how it feels to cough up blood

夏

血を吐くやうな　倦うさ、たゆけさ
今日の日も畑に陽は照り、麦に陽は照り
睡るがやうな悲しさに、み空をとほく
血を吐くやうな倦うさ、たゆけさ

空は燃え、畑はつづき
雲浮び、眩しく光り
今日の日も陽は炎ゆる、地は睡る
血を吐くやうなせつなさに。

嵐のやうな心の歴史は
終焉つてしまつたもののやうに
そこから繰れる一つの緒もないもののやうに
燃ゆる日の彼方に睡る。

私は残る、亡骸として——
血を吐くやうなせつなさかなしさ。

Image

I

Wind blew toward pine trees.
Gravel was crunching lonely underfoot.
The warm wind washed my brow
as faraway thoughts filled me with longing.

Once I'd settled down to rest,
waves could be heard crashing louder.
Stars invisible,
the sky was of dark cotton.

In a passing yawl,
a boatman said something to his wife.
—Those words were inaudible.

Waves could be heard crashing louder.

心象

I

松の木に風が吹き、
踏む砂利の音は寂しかつた。
暖い風が私の額を洗ひ
思ひははるかに、なつかしかつた。

腰をおろすと、
浪の音がひときは聞えた。
星はなく
空は暗い綿だつた。

とほりかかつた小舟の中で
船頭がその女房に向つて何かを云つた。
——その言葉は、聞きとれなかつた。

浪の音がひときはきこえた。

II

for all the past that's died away
tears flow
the castle wall dries
wind blows

grasses wave
over the hill   across the field
eternally
I wonder if a white angel will come

oh I want to die
oh I want to live
oh for all the past that's died away

tears flow
from the sky
wind blows

II

亡びたる過去のすべてに
涙湧く。
城の塀乾きたり
風の吹く

草靡く
丘を越え、野を渉り
憩ひなき
白き天使のみえ来ずや

あはれわれ死なんと欲す、
あはれわれ生きむと欲す
あはれわれ、亡びたる過去のすべてに

涙湧く。
み空の方より、
風の吹く

MICHIKO

みちこ

Michiko

Your breast is as the ocean.
Generously it swells.
Far sky, blue waves—
Even a cool wind blows,
Touching the pine tree tops,
And the shore whitely extends.

Your eyes reflect the sky
To its very limits.
Lapping waves, waves at the shore
Suddenly change their shape.
Not looking at them—ships under full and half sail,
You gaze on those heading out to sea.

And the beauty of your forehead.
Surprised by a noise,
Like an ox whose afternoon daydream
Is broken, you innocently,
Lightly and gracefully
Raise your head and then drop it down again.

Your delicate nape is a rainbow.
Powerless your child-like arms.
When the reel songs are sung and you dance to their
  lively tunes,
Into the ocean field pours a sunset of teary gold,
Offshore falls even further away, a silently
  flourishing expanse,
And I look up, thinking you might vanish into the sky.

みちこ

そなたの胸は海のやう
おほらかにこそうちあぐる。
はるかなる空、あをき浪、
涼しかぜさへ吹きそひて
松の梢をわたりつつ
磯白々とつづきけり。

またなが目にはかの空の
いやはてまでもうつしゐて
竝びくるなみ、渚なみ、
いとすみやかにうつろひぬ。
みるとしもなく、ま帆片帆
沖ゆく舟にみとれたる。

またその額のうつくしさ
ふと物音におどろきて
午睡の夢をさまされし
牡牛のごとも、あどけなく
かろやかにまたしとやかに
もたげられ、さてうち俯しぬ。

しどけなき、なれが頸は虹にして
ちからなき、嬰児ごとき腕して
絃うたあはせはやきふし、なれの踊れば、
海原はなみだぐましき金にして夕陽をたたへ
沖つ瀬は、いよとほく、かしこしづかに
　うるほへる
空になん、汝の息絶ゆるとわれはながめぬ。

To Ruined Sorrow . . .

today again a little snow
falls on ruined sorrow
today again even the wind
blows through ruined sorrow

ruined sorrow is
for example a fox's hide
on ruined sorrow
a little snow falls and it shrinks

ruined sorrow never
hopes nor wishes anything
ruined sorrow
in languor dreams of death

pitifully I fear
ruined sorrow
dusk and there's nothing I can do
against ruined sorrow . . .

汚れつちまつた悲しみに……

汚れつちまつた悲しみに
今日も小雪の降りかかる
汚れつちまつた悲しみに
今日も風さへ吹きすぎる

汚れつちまつた悲しみは
たとへば狐の革裘
汚れつちまつた悲しみは
小雪のかかつてちぢこまる

汚れつちまつた悲しみは
なにのぞむなくねがふなく
汚れつちまつた悲しみは
倦怠のうちに死を夢む

汚れつちまつた悲しみに
いたいたしくも怖気づき
汚れつちまつた悲しみに
なすところもなく日は暮れる……

Untitled

I

My dear, you're so good to me, and yet
I'm stubborn. After we parted last night,
I drank and spoke ill of a weak person. This morning,
I awoke recalling your kindness
and deploring my own filth. And so,
with no sense of self, I here confess, without shame,
dignity, or even honesty,
that I am driven mad by my own delusions.
Finally, my dear, I never try to consider
other people's feelings. Though you're so good to me,
I was obstinate and selfish like a child!
I wake up and, through this awful hangover,
with a sense of the cold morning outside,
think of your kindness, and remember the one I cursed.
And now I'm confused and sad
and admit this morning that I'm worthless!

無題

I

こひ人よ、おまへがやさしくしてくれるのに、
私は強情だ。ゆうべもおまへと別れてのち、
酒をのみ、弱い人に毒づいた。今朝
目が覚めて、おまへのやさしさを思ひ出しながら
私は私のけがらはしさを歎いてゐる。そして
正体もなく、今茲に告白をする、恥もなく、
品位もなく、かといつて正直さもなく
私は私の幻想に駆られて、狂ひ廻る。
人の気持ちをみようとするやうなことはつひになく、
こひ人よ、おまへがやさしくしてくれるのに、
私は頑なで、子供のやうに我儘だつた！
目が覚めて、宿酔の厭ふべき頭の中で、
戸の外の、寒い朝らしい気配を感じながら
私はおまへのやさしさを思ひ、また毒づいた人
　を思ひ出す。
そしてもう、私はなんのことだか分らなく悲しく、
今朝はもはや私がくだらない奴だと、自ら信ずる！

II

Hers is an honest heart!
Grown up rough and tumble,
she has lived all alone in the untidy world
where no one considers her feelings,
yet her heart is more
honest than mine, and stable.

She is beautiful. In a whirlpool world without rules,
she lives wisely and modestly.
Because the whirlpool world has so few rules,
at times the heart becomes weak, a bit unsettled,
yet never surrenders its last dignity—
she is beautiful and wise!

How her spirit once called for a kind heart!
But now even she despairs.
She only encounters the selfish and adolescent—
animals and children. Still, unknowingly,
she just thinks everyone is a gangster
and puts them down a little. The poor girl!

II

彼女の心は真つ直い！
彼女は荒々しく育ち、
たよりもなく、心を汲んでも
もらへない、乱雑な中に
生きてきたが、彼女の心は
私のより真つ直いそしてぐらつかない

彼女は美しい。わいだめもない世の渦の中に
彼女は賢くつつましく生きてゐる。
あまりにわいだめもない世の渦のために、
折に心が弱り、弱々しく躁ぎはするが、
而もなほ、最後の品位をなくしはしない
彼女は美しい、そして賢い！

嘗て彼女の魂が、どんなにやさしい心を
　もとめてゐたかは！
しかしいまではもう諦めてしまつてさへゐる。
我利々々で、幼稚な、獣や子供にしか、
彼女は出遇はなかつた。おまけに彼女はそれと
　識らずに、
唯、人といふ人が、みんなやくざなんだと
　思つてゐる。
そして少しはいぢけてゐる。彼女は可哀想だ！

III

In such a world of sad living, let not
your heart harden.
I want mine to draw close to you,
so let not your heart harden.

For when yours hardens, its eyes—
the soul's labor of words—are lost.
When calm, all men can share innate
beautiful dreams, and also their reasons.

I forget and abandon my heart, my soul,
seek beauty in a drunken, mad feeling.
How sad my world is.

Without the feelings that come severally to mind,
only the heart is eager to conquer others.
Nothing is more pathetic than such feverish scenery.

III

かくは悲しく生きん世に、なが心
かたくなにしてあらしめな。
われはわが、したしさにはあらんとねがへば
なが心、かたくなにしてあらしめな。

かたくなにしてあるときは、心に眼
魂に、言葉のはたらきあとを絶つ
なごやかにしてあらんとき、人みなは
　生れしながらの
うまし夢、またそがことわり分ち得ん。

おのが心も魂も忘れはて棄て去りて
悪酔の、狂ひ心地に美を索む
わが世のさまのかなしさや、

おのが心におのがじし湧きくるおもひもたずして、
人に勝らん心のみいそがはしき
熱を病む風景ばかりかなしきはなし。

IV

I think of you.
Into the sweet, calmly clear mind,
day and night I sink myself,
feeling like a sinner.

I do love you: I give it everything.
And though possibilities swarm my head,
thinking about them is fruitless,
so I will serve you with my life.

And since there is no other way
for me to find any hope or purpose,
it makes me happy to do so.

I'm happy—forgetting all the world's troubles,
without knowing anything, I'm
happy—because I can serve you!

IV

私はおまへのことを思つてゐるよ。
いとほしい、なごやかに澄んだ気持の中に、
昼も夜も浸つてゐるよ、
まるで自分を罪人ででもあるやうに感じて。

私はおまへを愛してゐるよ、精一杯だよ。
いろんなことが考へられもするが、考へられても
それはどうにもならないことだしするから、
私は身を棄ててお前に尽さうと思ふよ。

またさうすることのほかには、私にはもはや
希望も目的も見出せないのだから
さうすることは、私に幸福なんだ。

幸福なんだ、世の煩ひのすべてを忘れて、
いかなることとも知らないで、私は
おまへに尽せるんだから幸福だ！

V Happiness

Happiness is in the stable,
on the straw.
Happiness is understood
at a glance by the peaceful heart.

> The stubborn heart, miserable and cranky,
> turning its mind to
> the whirlwind of events and things,
> falls even deeper into misery.

Happiness is resting
and has things which need to be clarified
little by little.
Happiness is brimming with empathy.

> The stubborn heart lacks empathy,
> doesn't know what to do, only pursues advantage,
> feels depressed, irritable,
> is widely hated, and feels sorry for itself.

Thus, foremost, one should always try to be obedient.
Though rejection breeds willfulness,
learn, so that obedience is the only kind of learning,
to enhance one's dignity, to enrich one's work!

V　幸福

幸福は厩の中にゐる
藁の上に。
幸福は
和める心には一挙にして分る。

　　頑なの心は、不幸でいらいらして、
　　せめてめまぐるしいものや
　　数々のものに心を紛らす。
　　そして益々不幸だ。

幸福は、休んでゐる
そして明らかになすべきことを
少しづつ持ち、
幸福は、理解に富んでゐる。

　　頑なの心は、理解に欠けて、
　　なすべきをしらず、ただ利に走り、
　　意気銷沈して、怒りやすく、
　　人に嫌はれて、自らも悲しい。

されば人よ、つねにまづ従はんとせよ。
従ひて、迎へられんとには非ず、
従ふことのみ学びとなるべく、学びて
汝が品格を高め、そが働きの裕かとならんため！

The Advance of Night

for Seiichirō Utsumi

Night after night, as the evening deepens, I hear
  the neighborhood bathhouse drawing water.
Steam rises from the runoff . . .
  Long ago pitch black nights of Musashino.
Fog hangs in the air,
  the moon bright above,
and a dog is howling.

That's when I dream a tender
  dream beside the hearth.
Although it's mostly ruined now,
  my heart remains gentle.
On nights like this it gradually begins to murmur,
  and I listen to it thankfully,
I listen to it thankfully.

更くる夜

内海誓一郎に

毎晩々々、夜が更けると、近所の湯屋の
　水汲む音がきこえます。
流された残り湯が湯気となつて立ち、
　昔ながらの真つ黒い武蔵野の夜です。
おつとり霧も立罩めて
　その上に月が明るみます、
と、犬の遠吠がします。

その頃です、僕が囲炉裏の前で、
　あえかな夢をみますのは。
随分……今では損はれてはゐるものの
　今でもやさしい心があつて、
こんな晩ではそれが徐かに呟きだすのを、
　感謝にみちて聴きいるのです、
感謝にみちて聴きいるのです。

Sinner's Song

for Rokurō Abe

Sadness of my life, pruned too early
by inept gardeners!
Since then the bulk of my blood
has risen to my head, boiled, simmered.

Troubled, with a sense of urgency,
keep trying to reclaim the world below.
Such behavior is foolish,
such thought indivisible.

And so this pitiful tree,
rough bark exposed to sky and wind,
heart always sunk in mourning,

lazy, sporadic of gesture,
timid before others and quick to submit, then,
unexpectedly, does every possible stupid thing.

つみびとの歌

阿部六郎に

わが生は、下手な植木師らに
あまりに夙く、手を入れられた悲しさよ！
由来わが血の大方は
頭にのぼり、煮え返り、滾り泡だつ。

おちつきがなく、あせり心地に、
つねに外界に索めんとする。
その行ひは愚かで、
その考へは分ち難い。

かくてこのあはれなる木は、
粗硬な樹皮を、空と風とに、
心はたえず、追惜のおもひに沈み、

懶懦にして、とぎれとぎれの仕草をもち、
人にむかつては心弱く、諂ひがちに、かくて
われにもない、愚事のかぎりを仕出来してしまふ。

AUTUMN

秋

Autumn

1

The field which had until yesterday been aflame,
today spreads, vague, beneath a cloudy sky.
People say autumn deepens with each rain.
Already the autumn cicadas are singing,
amidst the grass, from a solitary tree.

I put a cigarette in my mouth. The smoke
rises, twisting into the stagnant air.
I cannot stare at the horizon even if I want to,
what with the rising and sinking of heat wave ghosts.
—So I can only crouch down.

Tinged with a dull gold, the sky is cloudy—it hasn't
  changed—
and because it is so high, I have to bow my head.
I resign myself to the boredom of living.
The smoke has triple flavors.
It seems I may be nearing the end of my life . . .

秋

I

昨日まで燃えてゐた野が
今日茫然として、曇つた空の下につづく。
一雨毎に秋になるのだ、と人は云ふ
秋蟬は、もはやかしこに鳴いてゐる、
草の中の、ひともとの木の中に。

僕は煙草を喫ふ。その煙が
澱んだ空気の中をくねりながら昇る。
地平線はみつめようにもみつめられない
陽炎の亡霊達が起つたり坐つたりしてゐるので、
——僕は蹲んでしまふ。

鈍い金色を帯びて、空は曇つてゐる、——相変らずだ、——
とても高いので、僕は俯いてしまふ。
僕は倦怠を観念して生きてゐるのだよ、
煙草の味が三通りくらゐにする。
死ももう、とほくはないのかもしれない……

II

"And then, saying goodbye,
strangely, wearing a smile filled with a kind of brassy
luster,
out that door he went.
The smile didn't seem like that of a living thing.

His eyes were the color of purified marsh water.
Whenever we talked, his mind seemed to be elsewhere.
He spoke in short bursts, pausing between phrases.
And trivial things—he remembered them in such detail."

"Yes, that's right. He knew he was going to die, didn't he?
When he saw a star the other day, he smiled, saying, that
star will be me.
. . . .
It was just the other day, and he kept saying his geta were
not his own."

geta: wooden sandals

II

『それではさよならといつて、
めうに真鍮の光沢かなんぞのやうな笑を湛へて
　彼奴は、
あのドアの所を立去つたのだつたあね。
あの笑ひがどうも、生きてる者のやうぢやなかつ
　たあね。

彼奴の目は、沼の水が澄んだ時かなんかのやう
　な色をしてたあね。
話してる時、ほかのことを考へてゐる
　やうだつたあね。
短く切つて、物を云ふくせがあつたあね。
つまらない事を、細かく覚えてたりしたあね。』

『ええさうよ。——死ぬつてことが分つてゐたのだ
　わ？
星をみてると、星が僕になるんだなんて笑つてた
　わよ、たつた先達よ。
………………………………………………………
たつた先達よ、自分の下駄を、これあどうしても
　僕のぢやないつていふのよ。』

III

The grass didn't move at all.
A butterfly flew above.
Dressed in a yukata, he stood watching it from the porch.
I kept an eye on how he was doing from over here.
He was gazing at the yellow butterfly.
There came the sound of the tofu peddler's horn;
that power pole rose clear against the evening sky.

—I, he turned to me and said,
dug up a two-hundred-and-fifty-pound stone yesterday.
—Well, but what for? Where? I asked him.
Then he stared into my eyes.
He looked angry, and, well . . . I got scared.

How strange one's last days are . . .

yukata: cotton summer kimono

III

草がちつともゆれなかつたのよ、
その上を蝶々がとんでゐたのよ。
浴衣を着て、あの人縁側に立つてそれを見てるのよ。
あたしこつちからあの人の様子　見てたわよ。
あの人ジッと見てるのよ、黄色い蝶々を。
お豆腐屋の笛が方々で聞こえてゐたわ、
あの電信柱が、夕空にクッキリしてて、

——僕、つてあの人あたしの方を振向くのよ、
昨日三十貫くらゐある石をコジ起しちやつた、つてのよ。
——まあどうして、どこで？つてあたし訊いたのよ。
するとね、あの人あたしの目をジッとみるのよ、
怒つてるやうなのよ、まあ……あたし怖かつたわ。

死ぬまへつてへんなものねえ……

Elegy for the Town of Shura

for Takakatsu Sekiguchi

First Song

Evil memories,
begone! And old
feelings of mercy,
heart of hearts,
come back to me!

  Today is Sunday.
  Sunlight falls across the porch.
  —Once again, I want mother to take me
  to buy a balloon at a festival.
  Blue sky, everything was bright and dazzling . . .

  Evil memories,
  begone!
    Gone, begone!

修羅街輓歌

関口隆克に

序歌

忌はしい憶ひ出よ、
去れ！　そしてむかしの
憐みの感情と
ゆたかな心よ、
返つて来い！

　今日は日曜日
　縁側には陽が当る。
　——もういつぺん母親に連れられて
　祭の日には風船玉が買つてもらひたい、
　空は青く、すべてのものはまぶしくかゞやかし
　　かつた……

　忌はしい憶ひ出よ、
　去れ！
　　去れ去れ！

II Drunk and Sober

Gone, also, is my youth.
—On this cold morning, a rooster's crow!
Gone, also, is my youth.

Yes, I've lived without a backward or forward glance . . .
Was I too cheerful?
—An innocent soldier, my heart!

Nevertheless, I hate
people who live with only an awareness of the outward.
—Paradoxical life.

Here, now, all broken down.
—On this cold morning, a rooster's crow!
O frost and rooster endlessly crowing . . .

III Soliloquy

One must be careful not to shake a basin of water:
how one carries the basin is important.
If this is so, then
big motions are best.

However, in doing so,
if you've no ingenuity left to spend . . .
heart,
be humble and wait for grace.

II 酔生

私の青春も過ぎた、
——この寒い明け方の鶏鳴よ！
私の青春も過ぎた。

ほんに前後もみないで生きて来た……
私はあむまり陽気にすぎた？
——無邪気な戦士、私の心よ！

それにしても私は憎む、
対外意識にだけ生きる人々を。
——パラドクサルな人生よ。

いま茲に傷つきはてて、
——この寒い明け方の鶏鳴よ！
おゝ、霜にしみらの鶏鳴よ……

III 独語

器の中の水が揺れないやうに、
器を持ち運ぶことは大切なのだ。
さうでさへあるならば
モーションは大きい程いい。

しかしさうするために、
もはや工夫を凝らす余地もないなら……
心よ、
謙抑にして神恵を待てよ。

IV

Today is such a pale day.
Rain falls bleakly
and the air, which is paler than water,
has a woodland smell.

A deep autumn day like today
has the sound of stones.
It's not even a memory,
let alone a dream.

Indeed, I haven't lived
like a stone or shadow.
Even if I try to shout, no words come—
nor an ending like the sky.

Yes, my heart is sorrowful.
For no reason I shake my fist,
and who can be blamed for that?
I am as sad as can be.

IV

いといと淡き今日の日は
雨蕭々と降り洒ぎ
水より淡き空気にて
林の香りすなりけり。

げに秋深き今日の日は
石の響きの如くなり。
思ひ出だにもあらぬがに
まして夢などあるべきか。

まことや我は石のごと
影の如くは生きてきぬ……
呼ばんとするに言葉なく
空の如くははてもなし。

それよかなしきわが心
いはれもなくて拳する
誰をか責むることかある？
せつなきことのかぎりなり。

Snowy Evening

Snow falling on a blue fedora
is the hand of the past, or whispering.

—Hakushu

Snow falling on the hotel roof
is the hand of the past, or whispering.

    A chimney belches smoke,
    and red sparks flurry.

Tonight the sky is pitch black,
and the snow falling from the black sky is . . .

    That woman I left, I really wonder
    how she's doing now.

That woman I left, I really wonder
if she will ever come back.

    I drink quietly,
    dipping into my regrets.

Quietly, quietly drink,
kindled by a longing . . .

    Snow falling on the hotel roof
    is the hand of the past, or whispering.

A chimney belches smoke,
and red sparks flurry.

雪の宵

青いソフトに降る雪は
過ぎしその手か囁きか　　白秋

ホテルの屋根に降る雪は
過ぎしその手か、囁きか

　　ふかふか煙突煙吐いて、
　　赤い火の粉も刎ね上る。

今夜み空はまつ暗で、
暗い空から降る雪は……

　　ほんに別れたあのをんな、
　　いまごろどうしてゐるのやら。

ほんにわかれたあのをんな、
いまに帰つてくるのやら

　　徐かに私は酒のんで
　　悔と悔とに身もそぞろ。

しづかにしづかに酒のんで
いとしおもひにそそらるる……

　　ホテルの屋根に降る雪は
　　過ぎしその手か、囁きか

ふかふか煙突煙吐いて
赤い火の粉も刎ね上る。

Song of Upbringing

I

infancy
the snow that fell on me
was like floss silk

childhood
the snow that fell on me
was like sleet

seventeen to nineteen
the snow that fell on me
dropped like hail

twenty to twenty-two
the snow that fell on me
seemed like balls of ice

twenty-three
the snow that fell on me
looked like a blizzard

twenty-four
the snow that fell on me
became so mournful

生ひ立ちの歌

I

　　幼年時
私の上に降る雪は
真綿のやうでありました

　　少年時
私の上に降る雪は
霙のやうでありました

　　十七―十九
私の上に降る雪は
霰のやうに散りました

　　二十―二十二
私の上に降る雪は
雹であるかと思はれた

　　二十三
私の上に降る雪は
ひどい吹雪とみえました

　　二十四
私の上に降る雪は
いとしめやかになりました……

II

the snow that falls on me
falls like petals
when the burning firewood makes a noise
and the frozen sky darkens

the snow that fell on me
so delicate and lovely
fell reaching out a hand

the snow that fell on me
was like tears
that sink into a burning forehead

to the snow that fell on me
I offered heartfelt thanks and prayed to God
that I would live a long life

the snow that fell on me
was so chaste

II

私の上に降る雪は
花びらのやうに降つてきます
薪の燃える音もして
凍るみ空の黝む頃

私の上に降る雪は
いとなよびかになつかしく
手を差伸べて降りました

私の上に降る雪は
熱い額に落ちもくる
涙のやうでありました

私の上に降る雪に
いとねんごろに感謝して、神様に
長生したいと祈りました

私の上に降る雪は
いと貞潔でありました

Now is the Hour . . .

Now is the hour when flowers exhale perfume like a censer.
—Baudelaire

Now is the hour when flowers exhale
perfume like a censer. Hazy atmosphere.
Flowers drip with dew.
Sounds of water, people hurrying home.

Truly, Yasuko, now is the hour
when we should sit quietly together.
Birds in the far sky
fill me with a touching sympathy.

Truly, Yasuko, now is the hour
when bamboo fences and a calm
expanse of cobalt sky flow quietly.

Truly, Yasuko, now is the hour
when your hair becomes supple,
when flowers exhale perfume like a censer,

時こそ今は……

時こそ今は花は香炉に打薫じ
ボードレール

時こそ今は花は香炉に打薫じ、
そこはかとないけはひです。
しほだる花や水の音や、
家路をいそぐ人々や。

いかに泰子、いまこそは
しづかに一緒に、をりませう。
遠くの空を、飛ぶ鳥も
いたいけな情け、みちてます。

いかに泰子、いまこそは
暮るる籬や群青の
空もしづかに流るころ。

いかに泰子、いまこそは
おまへの髪毛なよぶころ
花は香炉に打薫じ、

SHEEP SONGS

羊の歌

Sheep Song

for Yoshihiro Yasuhara

I Prayer

May I die face up!
May not this small chin become smaller still!
Yes, I am blamed for what I have
not felt—an invocation to death, I believe.
Ah, if only I look up!
Then, at least, I might be as one who feels everything.

羊の歌

安原喜弘に

I 祈り

死の時には私が仰向かんことを！
この小さな顎が、小さい上にも小さくならんことを！
それよ、私は私が感じ得なかつたことのために、
罰されて、死は来たるものと思ふゆゑ。
あゝ、その時私の仰向かんことを！
せめてその時、私も、すべてを感ずる者であら
　んことを！

II

O expectations, stale and dismal airs,
leave this body of mine!
I want nothing anymore but simplicity,
quiet, murmurs and order.

O acquaintances, grantors of dark disgrace,
do not wake me again!
I will endure my solitude,
arms seeming already useless.

O eyes that open doubtfully,
open eyes that stay motionless for a while,
ah, heart that believes in others more than itself,

O expectations, stale and dismal airs,
leave, leave this body of mine!
I enjoy nothing anymore but my wretched dreams.

II

思惑よ、汝　古く暗き気体よ、
わが裡より去れよかし！
われはや単純と静けき呟きと、
とまれ、清楚のほかを希はず。

交際よ、汝陰鬱なる汚濁の許容よ、
更めてわれを目覚ますことなかれ！
われはや孤寂に耐へんとす、
わが腕は既に無用の有に似たり。

汝、疑ひとともに見開く眼よ
見開きたるまゝに暫しは動かぬ眼よ、
あゝ、己の外をあまりに信ずる心よ、

それよ思惑、汝　古く暗き空気よ、
わが裡より去れよかし去れよかし！
われはや、貧しきわが夢のほかに興ぜず

III

My youth was nothing but a lowering storm
occasionally lanced by sudden sun.

Baudelaire

there was a nine-year-old child
the child was a girl
and as if the world's atmosphere were hers
as if she could lean on it
she tilted her head
when she spoke with me

I warmed myself at a kotatsu
she sat on the tatami
an exceptionally mild winter afternoon
my room aglow with sunlight
when she tilted her head
her earlobes seemed translucent

trusting me   fully at ease
the girl's heart was of an orange color
its warmth neither overflowed
nor shrank like a deer
I forgot everything then
and gently contemplated time

tatami: straw mat flooring

III

我が生は恐ろしい嵐のやうであつた、
其処此処に時々陽の光も落ちたとはいへ。
ボードレール

九歳の子供がありました
女の子供でありました
世界の空気が、彼女の有であるやうに
またそれは、凭つかかられるもののやうに
彼女は頸をかしげるのでした
私と話してゐる時に。

私は炬燵にあたつてゐました
彼女は畳に坐つてゐました
冬の日の、珍しくよい天気の午前
私の室には、陽がいつぱいでした
彼女が頸かしげると
彼女の耳朶　陽に透きました。

私を信頼しきつて、安心しきつて
かの女の心は蜜柑の色に
そのやさしさは氾濫するなく、かといつて
鹿のやうに縮かむこともありませんでした
私はすべての用件を忘れ
この時ばかりはゆるやかに時間を熟読翫味
しました。

IV

Even so, my heart is lonely.
Every night, alone in a boarding room,
thinking thoughtlessly about thought, a monotonous
and wretched heart's duet . . .

I hear the sound of a steam whistle
and think of travel, my childhood—
no, no, I don't think of childhood or travel,
but see what looks like travel, what looks like childhood . . .

My heart filled with thoughts is closed,
like a rusty hand box.
White lips, dry cheeks,
fade into the cold stillness . . .

The more I get used to it, the more I endure.
This painful solitude. Without
my realizing it they fall, sudden and strange,
tears that are no longer tears of love . . .

kotatsu: low, covered table with a heating element underneath, used in winter

IV

さるにても、もろに侘しいわが心
夜な夜なは、下宿の室に独りゐて
思ひなき、思ひを思ふ　単調の
つまし心の連弾よ……

汽車の笛聞こえもくれば
旅おもひ、幼き日をばおもふなり
いなよいなよ、幼き日をも旅をも思はず
旅とみえ、幼き日とみゆものをのみ……

思ひなき、おもひを思ふわが胸は
閉ざされて、醺生ゆる手匣にこそはさも似たれ
しらけたる脣、乾きし頬
酷薄の、これな寂莫にほとぶなり……

これやこの、慣れしばかりに耐へもする
さびしさこそはせつなけれ、みづからは
それともしらず、ことやうに、たまさかに
ながる涙は、人恋ふる涙のそれにもはや
　あらず……

Atrophy

For all men, there comes a time of languishing.
—Proverb

First, one must have a thirst.
—Catherine de Medici

I no longer woke with good will.
Waking brought the sorrow of ordinary thought,
so I dreamed instead with dark resolve.
(I could neither settle in
nor escape that place)
Then evening came, and I thought
this world is like an ocean.
I imagined a watery expanse at dusk,
where a haggard boatman rows
with unsteady hands.
Looking to see if there are any fish or not,
he passes by staring at the surface.

悴憔

Pour tout homme, il vient une époque où l'homme languit.
—Proverbe

Il faut d'abord avoir soif……
—Cathérine de Médecis

私はも早、善い意志をもつては目覚めなかつた
起きれば愁はしい　平常のおもひ
私は、悪い意志をもつてゆめみた……
（私は其処に安住したのでもないが、
其処を抜け出すことも叶はなかつた）
そして、夜が来ると私は思ふのだつた、
此の世は、海のやうなものであると。
私はすこししけてゐる宵の海をおもつた
其処を、やつれた顔の船頭は
おぼつかない手で漕ぎながら
獲物があるかあるまいことか
水の面を、にらめながらに過ぎてゆく

II

once I believed
love poems were foolish

now I read love poems
just for the sake of it

and yet at times I want
to reach a higher state of poetry

I don't know if that's right or wrong
but such a feeling persists anyway

and sometimes irritates me
provoking outrageous desires

once I believed
love poems were foolish

yet now I do nothing
but dream about love

II

昔　私は思つてゐたものだつた
恋愛詩なぞ愚劣なものだと

今私は恋愛詩を詠み
甲斐あることに思ふのだ

だがまだ今でもともすると
恋愛詩よりもましな詩境にはいりたい

その心が間違つてゐるかゐないか知らないが
とにかくさういふ心が残つてをり

それは時々私をいらだて
とんだ希望を起させる

昔私は思つてゐたものだつた
恋愛詩なぞ愚劣なものだと

けれどもいまでは恋愛を
ゆめみるほかに能がない

III

how am I to know if this
is my degradation or not

this arm-dangling indolence
the sun still shines today   blue sky

perhaps this idleness is all I have
ever been able to manage

or perhaps   I only yearned
for honest desires because I was idle

ah even so even so
I have never thought to be   a man who only dreams!

III

それが私の堕落かどうか
どうして私に知れようものか

腕にたるむだ私の怠惰
今日も日が照る　空は青いよ

ひよつとしたなら昔から
おれの手に負へたのはこの怠惰だけだつたかも
　しれぬ

真面目な希望も　その怠惰の中から
憧憬したのにすぎなかつたかもしれぬ

あゝ　それにしてもそれにしても
ゆめみるだけの　男にならうとはおもはなかつた！

IV

nevertheless the good and evil of this world
are not easily understood by humanity

countless reasons that we cannot fathom
govern every little thing

it's just fun if you're patient and persevere
like spring water in mountain shade

I believe all that is visible from the train
mountains grass the sky river everything

will soon melt into complete harmony
and rise into the blue to form a rainbow

IV

しかし此の世の善だの悪だの
容易に人間に分りはせぬ

人間に分らない無数の理由が
あれをもこれをも支配してゐるのだ

山蔭の清水のやうに忍耐ぶかく
つぐむでゐれば愉しいだけだ

汽車からみえる　山も　草も
空も　川も　みんなみんな

やがては全体の調和に溶けて
空に昇つて　虹となるのだらうとおもふ……

V

Now, how to turn a profit,
how to avoid losing face.

I mean, you people who spend all your time
on such things, making demands of others,

I used to think your attitude was reasonable
and eagerly went right along with you,

but today I will come to my senses again,
like a rubber band snapping back.

And so, within this window of indolence,
I spread my fingers in the shape of a fan,

savor the blue sky and drink peace,
floating like a frog on water.

Night being night, I watch the stars.
Ah, depths of the sky, depths of the sky.

V

さてどうすれば利するだらうか、とかと
どうすれば哂はれないですむだらうか、とかと

要するに人を相手の思惑に
明けくれすぐす、世の人々よ、

僕はあなたがたの心も尤もと感じ
一生懸命郷に従つてもみたのだが

今日また自分に帰るのだ
ひつぱつたゴムを手離したやうに

さうしてこの怠惰の窗の中から
扇のかたちに食指をひろげ

青空を喫ふ　閑を嚥む
蛙さながら水に泛んで

夜は夜とて星をみる
あゝ　空の奥、空の奥。

VI

But this condition persists.
Although I believe I must behave as others do,
I feel myself small,
and am even shocked by a department store delivery boy.

And although the reason is always clear—
trash, trash, trash of disbelief at the bottom of my heart.
However absurd it seems, these two
no doubt consist in me eternally, can never fall away.

Drawn to the sound of music,
I feel revived a little,
but the moment those two die within me—

ah, songs of sky and ocean,
I think I know the very essence of beauty,
and yet how hard it is to have no way of shaking off
 my idleness!

VI

しかし　またかうした僕の状態がつづき、僕とても何か人のするやうなことをしなければならないと思ひ、
自分の生存をしんきくさく感じ、
ともすると百貨店のお買上品届け人にさへ驚嘆する。

そして理窟はいつでもはつきりしてゐるのに
気持の底ではゴミゴミゴミゴミ懐疑の小屑が一杯です。
それがばかげてゐるにしても、その二つつが
僕の中にあり、僕から抜けぬことはたしかなのです

と、聞えてくる音楽には心惹かれ、
ちよつとは生き生きしもするのですが、
その時その二つつは僕の中に死んで、

あゝ　空の歌、海の歌、
僕は美の、核心を知つてゐるとおもふのですが
それにしても辛いことです、怠惰を逭れるすべがない！

Voice of Life

All my many deeds, how they wane beneath the sun.
—Solomon

I'm fed up with Bach and Mozart.
Had it altogether with that happy, superficial jazz.
I live like an iron bridge under a cloudy sky after it rains.
I'm pressed by things that are and always will be desolate.

I'm not completely still in the midst of such desolation.
I'm in search of something, constantly in search of
something.
Although frozen in this terrible state of inertia, I'm also
terribly impatient.
For the sake of which, appetites for food and sex are
as nothing.

However, what that thing is I don't know, nor have I
ever known.
I don't think there are two of them: I think there may
only be one.
But what that thing is I don't know, nor have I ever
known.
Not even how to have so much as a one-in-eight chance
of getting it have I ever known.

いのちの声

もろもろの業、太陽のもとにては蒼ざめたるかな。
——ソロモン

僕はもうバッハにもモツアルトにも倦果てた。
あの幸福な、お調子者のヂャズにもすつかり倦
　果てた。
僕は雨上りの曇つた空の下の鉄橋のやうに
　生きてゐる。
僕に押寄せてゐるものは、何時でもそれは寂漠だ。

僕はその寂漠の中にすつかり沈静してゐる
　わけでもない。
僕は何かを求めてゐる、絶えず何かを求めてゐる。
恐ろしく不動の形の中にだが、また恐ろしく
　憔れてゐる。
そのためにははや、食慾も性慾もあつてなきが
　如くでさへある。

しかし、それが何かは分らない、つひぞ分つた
　ためしはない。
それが二つあるとは思へない、ただ一つである
　とは思ふ。
しかしそれが何かは分らない、つひぞ分つた
　ためしはない。
それに行き著く一か八かの方途さへ、悉皆
　分つたためしはない。

Sometimes I ask, as though kidding myself,
Is it a woman? Something sweet? Or is it honor?
Then my heart screams, It isn't that! It isn't this! It's
neither that nor this!
Then is it a song of the sky—a sky song that echoes,
mornings, through the stratosphere?

2

No matter what, it cannot be described!
Sometimes I only want to describe it briefly,
but even though it remains indescribable, I still believe
my life is worth living.
Oh, that's reality! Undefiled joy! Which is to say,
just take whatever comes as it is!

Everyone, whether he realizes it or not, has this hope,
although it's not as simple as victory or defeat:
it's a kind of blissful daze that everyone knows,
everyone desires,
and yet no one can ever fully attain it while they're in
this world!

However, if happiness is like this, the limits of asceticism,
if it is something these wily merchants regard as the pit
of stupidity,
then the real world, where it is impossible to live
without food,
must be called unfair.

時に自分を揶揄ふやうに、僕は自分に訊いて
　みるのだ。
それは女か？　甘いものか？　それは栄誉か？
すると心は叫ぶのだ、あれでもない、これでも
　ない、あれでもないこれでもない！
それでは空の歌、朝、高空に、鳴響く空の歌と
　でもいふのであらうか？

二

否何れとさへそれはいふことの出来ぬもの！
手短かに、時に説明したくなるとはいふものの、
説明なぞ出来ぬものでこそあれ、我が生は
　生くるに値ひするものと信ずる
それよ現実！　汚れなき幸福！　あらはる
　ものはあらはるまゝによいといふこと！

人は皆、知ると知らぬに拘らず、そのことを希望
　してをり、
勝敗に心覚き程は知るによしないものであれ、
　それは誰も知る、放心の快感に似て、誰もが
　望み
誰もがこの世にある限り、完全には望み得ない
　もの！

併し幸福といふものが、このやうに無私の境の
　ものであり、
かの慧敏なる商人の、称して阿呆といふでも
　あらう底のものとすれば、
めしをくはねば生きてゆかれぬ現身の世は、
　不公平なものであるよといはねばならぬ。

But that's the world all the same,
and here we live, and it's not arbitrary injustice:
if it is the principle on which we are made,
then we can rest for a while, because there are no
extremes in the world.

3

In the end, it comes down to passion.
Thou, if thou dost boil over with anger from the bottom
of thy heart,
then rage!

Getting angry is natural, so that,
even if thou art nearing thy ultimate goal,
never, never neglect this word.

Thy passion will endure for a time and then subside,
but the effect on society will remain
and become a hindrance to changing thy conduct
henceforth.

4

Evening, under the sky, feeling the singularity of self, one
has no complaints about anything.

だが、それが此の世といふものなんで、其処に
　我等は生きてをり、それは任意の不公平
　ではなく、
それに因て我等自身も構成されたる原理であれば、
　然らば、この世に極端はないとて、一先づ
　休心するもよからう。

三

されば要は、熱情の問題である。
汝、心の底より立腹せば
怒れよ！

さあれ、怒ることこそ
汝が最後なる目標の前にであれ、
この言ゆめゆめおろそかにする勿れ。

そは、熱情はひととき持続し、やがて熄むなるに、
その社会的効果は存続し、
汝が次なる行為への転調の障げとなるなれば。

四

ゆふがた、空の下で、身一点に感じられれば、
　万事に於て文句はないのだ。

Songs of
Bygone Days
在りし日の歌

Dedicated to the spirit of my late son, Fumiya

亡き児文也の霊に捧ぐ

Shame

—A Song of Bygone Days—

Why do I feel so ashamed?
Autumn, and a mountain in shadow on a cold windy day.
In the hollows of the dead chestnut leaves,
the tree trunks stood oddly mature.

Around the corners of the branches, the sad sky was filled
with the ghosts of dead children, and I blinked.
But far away above the fields
was the dream of an ancient elephant patching
an Astrakhan coat.

In the hollows of the dead chestnut leaves,
the tree trunks stood oddly mature.
That day, in the gaps between trunks, your eyes
were intimate, the color of an older sister's.

That day, in the gaps between trunks, your eyes
were intimate, the color of an older sister's.
Ah! Still faintly glowing, the burn of bygone days.
Why, why is my heart so ashamed . . .

含羞

——在りし日の歌——

なにゆゑに　こゝろかくは羞ぢらふ
秋　風白き日の山かげなりき
椎の枯葉の落窪に
幹々は　いやにおとなびイちゐたり

枝々の　拱みあはすあたりかなしげの
空は死児等の亡霊にみち　まばたきぬ
をりしもかなた野のうへは
あすとらかんのあはひ縫ふ　古代の象の夢なりき

椎の枯葉の落窪に
幹々は　いやにおとなびイちゐたり
その日　その幹の隙　睦みし瞳
姉らしき色　きみはありにし

その日　その幹の隙　睦みし瞳
姉らしき色　きみはありにし
あゝ！　過ぎし日の　仄燃えあざやぐをりをりは
わが心　なにゆゑに　なにゆゑにかくは
　羞ぢらふ……

Emptiness

falling in the street that year-end festival night
  heart caught in a barbed wire fence
greasy bust open to the world
  with nothing to lean on me a streetwalker

so sad that I am unable to cry
  these days full of darkness
streaks echo across the faraway sky
  a coastal strait winter dawn breeze

artificial white rose petals
  frozen having lost all heart
this company of maidens on their big day off
  all of them my longtime sisters

rhomboids=tangential surfaces touch
  but still the Chinese fiddle continues to play

むなしさ

臘祭の夜の　巷に堕ちて
　心臓はも　条網に絡み
脂ぎる　胸乳も露は
　よすがなき　われは戯女

せつなきに　泣きも得せずて
　この日頃　闇を孕めり
遐き空　線条に鳴る
　海峡岸　冬の暁風

白薔薇の　造化の花弁
　凍てつきて　心もあらず
明けき日の　乙女の集ひ
　それらみな　ふるのわが友

偏菱形＝聚接面そも
　胡弓の音　つづきてきこゆ

Late Night Rain

—Image of Verlaine—

The rain is singing its old song tonight,
    just the same as always.
It drags on and on, insistent.
  And then I see Mr. Ver's figure
walking along the road between the warehouses.

Between roadside warehouses, his rubber raincoat's reflection.
    And then the peat-soaked magic tricks.
Now, if I can get past this road,
    if I can just get past it, I'll have a faint hope . . .
Isn't that a kind of hope, after all?

There's no need for automobiles,
    much less glaring streetlights.
Rotten eyeballs of tavern lamps,
    and bells are ringing far away.

夜更の雨

——ヹルレーヌの面影——

雨は　今宵も　昔　ながらに、
　　昔　ながらの　唄を　うたつてる。
だらだら　だらだら　しつこい　程だ。
　と、見る　ヹル氏の　あの図体が、
倉庫の　間の　路次を　ゆくのだ。

倉庫の　間にや　護謨合羽の　反射だ。
　　それから　泥炭の　しみたれた　巫戯けだ。
さてこの　路次を　抜けさへ　したらば、
　　抜けさへ　したらと　ほのかな
　　のぞみだ……
いやはや　のぞみにや　相違も　あるまい？

自動車　なんぞに　用事は　ないぞ、
　　あかるい　外燈なぞは　なほの　ことだ。
酒場の　軒燈の　腐つた　眼玉よ、
　　遐くの　方では　舎密も　鳴つてる。

Early Spring Wind

another day of golden wind
a silver bell in the big wind
another day of golden wind

like a queen's crown
I sit before a table
facing a wide window

the wind outside is golden wind
a silver bell in the big wind
another day of golden wind

the dry grass makes a sad sound
as smoke plays rough with the sky
and shadows happily bloom and fade

when I cross dark brown soil
laundry poles stretch into the sky
the hill road I climb is calm

like a young woman's chin
thorny treetops on the hill
another golden wind today . . .

早春の風

　　けふ一日また金の風
　大きい風には銀の鈴
けふ一日また金の風

　　女王の冠さながらに
　卓の前には腰を掛け
かびろき窓にむかひます

　　外吹く風は金の風
　大きい風には銀の鈴
けふ一日また金の風

　　枯草の音のかなしくて
　煙は空に身をすさび
日影たのしく身を嫋ぶ

　　鳶色の土かをるれば
　物干竿は空に往き
登る坂道なごめども

　　青き女の顎かと
　岡に梢のとげとげし
今日一日また金の風……

Moon

Tonight's moon has gorged itself.
Doubtful the biwa from the chemical factory roof
  will play.
The smell of lime can't scare me.
Shrubs are sharpening their individuality.
The sisters slept; their mother closed the crimson lattice!

Now, on the balcony,
if you look, you'll see a copper coin falling—or maybe
  it's a medal?
It must belong to Fumiko-san, who dropped it
  this afternoon.
I'll deliver it tomorrow.
I put it in my pocket, but it bothers me. Tonight's moon
  has gorged itself.
Shrubs are sharpening their individuality.
The sisters slept; the mother closed the crimson lattice!

biwa: Japanese short-necked lute, sometimes played to accompany traditional storytelling

月

今宵月は襄食を食ひ過ぎてゐる
済製場の屋根にブラ下つた琵琶は鳴るとしも
　想へぬ
石灰の匂ひがしたつて怖けるには及ばぬ
灌木がその個性を砥いでゐる
姉妹は眠つた、母親は紅殻色の格子を締めた！

さてベランダの上にだが
見れば銅貨が落ちてゐる、いやメダルなのかア
これは今日昼落とした文子さんのだ
明日はこれを届けてやらう
ポケットに入れたが気にかゝる。月は襄荷を
　食ひ過ぎてゐる
灌木がその個性を砥いでゐる
姉妹は眠つた、母親は紅殻色の格子を締めた！

Blue Eyes

1. Summer Morning

Night dawned in a sad heart.
    Night dawned in a happy heart.
No, what's the matter with this?
    Anyway, a sad night dawns!

The blue eyes didn't move.
    All the world was still asleep.
And so "that time" was passing on—
    oh, a story far, far away.

The blue eyes didn't move
—maybe they're moving now . . .
The blue eyes didn't move,
    lovely for being pitiful!

I'm here now, in the yellow firelight.
    I don't know what happened afterwards . . .
Oh, that's how "that time" was passing on!
    Blue, like gushing steam.

青い瞳

1 夏の朝

かなしい心に夜が明けた、
　　うれしい心に夜が明けた、
いいや、これはどうしたといふのだ？
　　さてもかなしい夜の明けだ！

青い瞳は動かなかつた、
　　世界はまだみな眠つてゐた、
さうして「その時」は過ぎつつあつた、
　　ああ、遐い遐いい話。

青い瞳は動かなかつた、
　　——いまは動いてゐるかもしれない……
青い瞳は動かなかつた、
　　いたいたしくて美しかつた！

私はいまは此処にゐる、黄色い灯影に。
　　あれからどうなつたのかしらない……
あゝ『あの時』はあゝして過ぎつゝあつた！
　　碧い噴き出す蒸気のやうに。

2. Winter Morning

What happened afterwards . . .
That I didn't know.
Anyway, the plane had vanished forever
from the airport shrouded in morning fog.
All that was left were cruel pebbles, weeds,
and a cold that split your cheeks.
—Even on such a cruel and vast morning,
people still have to greet each other with a smile.
It seemed like such a pathetic thing to do,
and yet, even there,
those who smiled the most
felt superior.
Sun struck the fog, frost melted off the grass,
a rooster crowed from a faraway house,
but the fog, sunlight, frost and rooster
did not touch people's hearts,
and they all went home and sat down to eat.
        (The last one left at the airport,
        I kick at an empty pack of Golden Bats.)

Golden Bats: a cheap and popular brand of cigarettes

2. 冬の朝

それからそれがどうなつたのか……
それは僕には分らなかつた
とにかく朝霧罩めた飛行場から
機影はもう永遠に消え去つていた。
あとには残酷な砂礫だの、雑草だの
頬を裂るような寒さが残つた。
——こんな残酷な空寞たる朝にも猶
人は人に笑顔を以て対さねばならないとは
なんとも情ないことに思はれるのだつたが
それなのに其処でもまた
笑いを沢山湛へた者ほど
優越を感じてゐるのであった。
陽は霧に光り、草葉の霜は解け、
遠くの民家に鶏は鳴いたが、
霧も光も霜も鶏も
みんな人々の心には沁まず、
人々は家に帰って食卓についた。
　　（飛行場に残つたのは僕、
　　バットの空箱を蹴つてみる）

Memory From the Age of Three

When sun shines on the porch
and resin sleeps in its five shades,
in the garden with one persimmon tree,
the soil is a loquat color and flies buzz.

I was held over my chamber pot,
and a roundworm fell from my bottom.
I was amazed to see it
move around in the shallow pot.

Ahh, that was really scary,
was strangely scary,
and I cried myself out
just because I wanted to.

Ah, it was scary, so scary.
—Inside the room was silent,
but the house next door was flying away into the sky!
The house next door was flying away into the sky!

三歳の記憶

緑側に陽があたつてて、
樹脂が五彩に眠る時、
柿の木いつぽんある中庭は、
土は枇杷いろ　蝿が唸く。

稚厠の上に　抱へられてた、
すると尻から　蛔虫が下がつた。
その蛔虫が、稚厠の浅瀬で動くので
動くので、私は吃驚しちまつた。

あゝあ、ほんとに怖かつた
なんだか不思議に怖かつた、
それでわたしはひとしきり
ひと泣き泣いて　やつたんだ。

あゝ、怖かつた怖かつた
——部屋の中は　ひつそりしてゐて、
隣家は空に　舞ひ去つてゐた！
隣家は空に　舞ひ去つてゐた！

June Rain

once again a morning rain
the green color of irises
a woman with glossy eyes and a slender face
blooms into view and fades

when she appears and fades
I quietly sink sink into joy
falling onto a field
I might be falling forever

beats a drum blows a flute
an innocent child Sunday
he plays on the tatami

beats a drum blows a flute
when he plays it rains
beyond the lattice window rain falls

六月の雨

またひとしきり　午前の雨が
菖蒲のいろの　みどりいろ
眼うるめる　面長き女
たちあらはれて　消えてゆく

たちあらはれて　消えゆけば
うれひに沈み　しとしとと
畠の上に　落ちてゐる
はてしもしれず　落ちてゐる

　　お太鼓叩いて　笛吹いて
　　あどけない子が　日曜日
　　畳の上で　遊びます

　　お太鼓叩いて　笛吹いて
　　遊んでゐれば　雨が降る
　　櫺子の外に　雨が降る

Rainy Day

Rain pours down on the street.
The houses' siding is old.
People's mocking eyes have become gentle,
and I awake from a flowery dream.

*

Old kite-brown sword sheath;
childhood friend with too much tongue
and a square forehead.
I remember you.

*

The rasp of a file, a husky voice,
and a tired old stomach.
Listen carefully in the rain
to those gentle, gentle lips.

*

The rainy sky blurs
a brick-colored desperation.
I miss that clever girl's black hair
and her loving father's head . . .

雨の日

通りに雨は降りしきり、
家々の腰板古い。
もろもろの愚弄の眼は淑やかとなり、
わたくしは、花弁の夢をみながら目を覚ます。

*

鳶色の古刀の鞘よ、
舌あまりの幼な友達、
おまへの額は四角張つてた。
わたしはおまへを思ひ出す。

*

鑪の音よ、だみ声よ、
老い疲れたる胃袋よ、
雨の中にはとほく聞け、
やさしいやさしい唇を。

*

煉瓦の色の憔心の
見え匿れする雨の空。
賢い少女の黒髪と、
慈父の首と懐かしい……

Spring

Spring makes the earth and grass shed new sweat.
To dry that sweat, larks soar into the sky.
This morning, the tiled roofs don't complain,
and a chorus rises from the long school building.

Ah, it's quiet. So quiet.
My spring of the year has come around again.
The hope that once filled my heart falls
on me from a sky become a deep, solemn blue.

And I am amazed, turn stupid
—what's that in the shade of bushes: a stream, silver,
  or ripples?
In the shade of bushes, is it a stream, silver, or ripples?

A big cat turns its neck
and clumsily rolls a bell.
Watching as it rolls a bell.

春

春は土と草とに新しい汗をかゝせる。
その汗を乾かさうと、雲雀は空に臓る。
瓦屋根今朝不平がない、
長い校舎から合唱は空にあがる。

あゝ、しづかだしづかだ。
めぐり来た、これが今年の私の春だ。
むかし私の胸摶つた希望は今日を、
厳めしい紺青となつて空から私に降りかゝる。

そして私は呆気てしまふ、バカになつてしまふ
——薮かげの、小川か銀か小波か？
薮かげの小川か銀か小波か？

大きい猫が頸ふりむけてぶきつちよに
一つの鈴をころばしてゐる、
一つの鈴を、ころばして見てゐる。

Song for a Spring Day

This flow a dim flirtation,
is it flowing into the country of the sky?
My heart is in utter shambles.
Egyptian cigarette smoke drifts up.

This cold and melancholy flow,
will it reach the foot of the mountain?
The point where one can just make out
the mysterious throat of a yet invisible face . . .

In the richness of a daydream,
in the sky in the sky above the field?
Wow. Wow. Am I not going to cry?

Until one can see beyond the yellow barn,
white warehouse the waterwheel,
will it not continue flowing flowing on?

春の日の歌

流よ、淡き　嬌羞よ、
ながれて　ゆくか　空の国?
心も　とほく　散らかりて、
ヱヂプト煙草　たちまよふ。

流よ、冷たき　憂ひ秘め、
ながれて　ゆくか　麓までも?
まだみぬ　顔の　不可思議の
咽喉の　みえる　あたりまで……

午睡の　夢の　ふくよかに、
野原の　空の　空のうへ?
うわあ　うわあと　涕くなるか

黄色い　納屋や、白の倉、
水車の　みえる　彼方まで、
ながれ　ながれて　ゆくなるか?

Summer Night

Ah, a cherry blossom woman
passes through my weary heart.
A woman goes by.

Dregs of rice fields on a summer night.
Resentment lingers.
—Will it reach the mountains that circle the basin?

Bare feet are gentle, the bottom is sandy,
and open eyes get left behind.
A foggy night sky high and black.

The foggy night sky is high and black,
and a parent's affections can do nothing.
—A petal passes through my weary heart.

A petal passes through my weary heart,
and a gong occasionally beats within.
The fog is beautiful, but it's hot!

夏の夜

あゝ　疲れた胸の裡を
桜色の　女が通る
女が通る。

夏の夜の水田の滓、
怨恨は気が遐くなる
——盆地を繞る山は巡るか？

裸足はやさしく　砂は底だ、
開いた瞳は　おいてきぼりだ、
霧の夜空は　高くて黒い。

霧の夜空は高くて黒い、
親の慈愛はどうしやうもない、
——疲れた胸の裡を　花弁が通る。

疲れた胸の裡を　花弁が通る
ときどき銅鑼が著物に触れて。
靄はきれいだけれども、暑い！

Song of the Young Beast

On a black night in a grassy field,
a beast struck a flint
in a fire pot and made a star.
Winter stirs and the wind howls.

The beast saw nothing anymore.
Embracing castanets, moonlight,
and other stars that will never wake up,
the urn welcomed blasphemy in.

Like after a rain, memories became one,
joined forces with the wind and struck the waves.
Oh, what a seductive story—
even slaves are as lovely as queens.

An aristocrat's eggshell smile
and the white blood cells of a retarded child,
these are what frighten the beast.

On a black night in a grassy field,
the beast's heart smolders.
On a black night in a grassy field—
Long ago, talking to oneself was also beautiful! . . .

幼獣の歌

黒い夜草深い野にあつて、
一匹の獣が火消壺の中で
燧石を打つて、星を作つた。
冬を混ぜる　風が鳴つて。

獣はもはや、なんにも見なかつた。
カスタニェットと月光のほか
目覚ますことなき星を抱いて、
壺の中には冒瀆を迎へて。

雨後らしく思い出は一塊となつて
風と肩を組み、波を打つた。
あゝ　なまめかしい物語——
奴隷も王女と美しかれよ。

　　卵殻もどきの貴公子の微笑と
　　遲鈍な子供の白血球とは、
　　それな獣を怖がらす。

黒い夜草深い野の中で、
一匹の獣の心は燻る。
黒い夜草深い野の中で——
太古は、独語も美しかつた！……

The Child

When cobalt sways the sky,
in the field
there is a pale
little child.

When black clouds draw lines in the sky,
the child
sheds tears that
are liquid silver . . .

I wish the world would split in two
and one half would modernize.
Then, I would sit down on the other side and gaze
at the blue sky all day—

Granite boulders.
Beach sky.
A temple roof
and the edge of the sea . . .

この小児

コボルト空に往交へば、
野に
蒼白の
この小児。

黒雲空にすぢ引けば、
この小児
絞る涙は
銀の液……

　　地球が二つに割れゝばいい、
　　そして片方は洋行すればいい、
　　すれば私はもう片方に腰掛けて
　　青空をばかり——

花崗の巖や
浜の空
み寺の屋根や
海の果て……

Winter Day Memory

One afternoon in a cold wind, a child picked up a sparrow
and loved it.
But that night he suddenly died.

The next morning a frost fell.
The child's big brother went to send a telegram.

Even at night, the mother cried.
The father was on a long sea voyage.

No one knew what happened to the sparrow.
The north wind was whitening the main road.

By chance, when they heard the sound of a well bucket,
word came back from the father.

Frost fell every day.
He would still be unable to return from his long sea voyage.

No one knows what the mother's been doing since then . . .
The brother who sent the telegram was scolded at
school today.

冬の日の記憶

昼、寒い風の中で雀を手にとつて愛してゐた
　子供が、
夜になつて、急に死んだ。

次の朝は霜が降つた。
その子の兄が電報打ちに行つた。

夜になつても、母親は泣いた。
父親は、遠洋航海してゐた。

雀はどうなつたか、誰も知らなかつた。
北風は往還を白くしてゐた。

つるべの音が偶々した時、
父親からの、返電が来た。

毎日々々霜が降つた。
遠洋航海からはまだ帰れまい。

その後母親がどうしてゐるか……
電報打つた兄は、今日学校で叱られた。

Autumn Day

passing through tree shade of river shoals
autumn is a beautiful woman's eyelids
it could rain it seems the sky is humid
sound of a bygone horse's hooves

for one who is tired from long years
take the main road and autumn really sinks in
if you don't realize it's there it's nothing after all
to be moved by at least the sound of wooden clogs

the sun now shines on half the shoals
an intangible raft floats along the stream
wildgrass leaning down on the far side

even my companion's foolish atmosphere
blends mysteriously into the mood
autumn worries lips are sewn shut

秋の日

　磧づたひの　竝樹の　蔭に
秋は　美し　女の　瞼
　泣きも　いでなん　空の　潤み
昔の　馬の　蹄の　音よ

　長の　年月　疲れの　ために
国道　いゆけば　秋は　身に沁む
　なんでも　ないてば　なんでも　ないに
木履の　音さへ　身に　沁みる

　陽は今　磧の　半分に　射し
流れを　無形の　筏は　とほる
　野原は　向ふで　伏せつて　ゐるが

連れだつ　友の　お道化た　調子も
　不思議に　空気に　溶け　込んで
秋は　案じる　くちびる　結んで

Icy Night

On a winter night
my heart is feeling sad,
sad for no reason . . .
A rusty purple heart.

Behind a solid door,
the old days are a blur.
On top of the hill,
cottonseeds burst open.

Here, firewood is smoldering,
and the smoke rises
as though it knows itself.

Being neither drawn to
nor in search of anything,
my heart smolders . . .

冷たい夜

冬の夜に
私の心が悲しんでゐる
悲しんでゐる、わけもなく……
心は錆びて、紫色をしてゐる。

丈夫な扉の向ふに、
古い日は放心してゐる。
丘の上では
棉の実が罅裂ける。

此処では薪が燻つてゐる、
その煙は、自分自らを
知つてでもゐるやうにのぼる。

誘はれるでもなく
覓めるでもなく、
私の心が燻る……

Winter Dawn

Lingering snow thin and hard on the roof tiles
makes branches drowsy like a deer.
At six o'clock on a winter morning,
my head, too, is asleep.

A crow caws as it flies by—
The garden ground also sleeps like a deer.
—The forest has fled, the farmer has fled,
and the sky is sad and weak.
        My heart is sad . . .

Eventually the sun shines
and the blue sky opens.
Above the stratosphere, Jupiter thunders his guns.
—The mountains on all sides sink,

the farmer's garden yawns,
and the road greets the sky.
        My heart is sad . . .

冬の明け方

残んの雪が瓦に少なく固く
枯木の小枝が鹿のやうに睡い、
冬の朝の六時
私の頭も睡い。

鳥が啼いて通る——
庭の地面も鹿のやうに睡い。
——林が逃げた農家が逃げた、
空は悲しい衰弱。
　　私の心は悲しい……

やがて薄日が射し
青空が開く。
上の上の空でジュピター神の砲が鳴る。
——四方の山が沈み、

農家の庭が欠伸をし、
道は空へと挨拶する。
　　私の心は悲しい……

As an Old Man

—"Empty Autumn" No. 12

Let the aged live in tranquility,
that they may regret to their hearts' content.

I want to regret.
Regretting to your heart's content is truly to rest the soul.

Oh, how I wish I could weep endlessly,
forgetting my father, mother, siblings, friends, and
   even strangers.

Like the dawn sky, an evening wind across the hills,
a fluttering flag, I could weep.

Or like words of goodbye that echo in the clouds,
   the fields,
that blend with the wind above the sea and pass on . . .

Tanka

Ah, because of our complacency, for a long time, a very long time, we've been so caught up in trifles that we've forgotten how to weep. Truly forgotten . . .

[The twenty-odd poems of "Empty Autumn" have been lost and no longer exist. Only the twelfth remains, thanks to Saburō Moroi's composition.]

老いたる者をして

——「空しき秋」第十二

老いたる者をして静謐の裡にあらしめよ
そは彼等こころゆくまで悔いんためなり

吾は悔いんことを欲す
こころゆくまで悔ゆるは洵に魂を休むればなり

あゝ　はてしもなく涕かんことこそ望ましけれ
父も母も兄弟も友も、はた見知らざる人々をも
　忘れて

東明の空の如く丘々をわたりゆく夕べの風の如く
はたなびく小旗の如く涕かんかな

或はまた別れの言葉の、こだまし、雲に入り、
　野末にひびき
海の上への風にまじりてとことはに過ぎ
　ゆく如く……

反歌

あゝ　吾等怯懦のために長き間、いとも長き間
徒なることにかゝらひて、涕くことを忘れゐたりし
よ、げに忘れゐたりしよ……

〔空しき秋二十数篇は散佚して今はなし。その
第十二のみ、諸井三郎の作曲によりて残りしもの
なり。〕

On the Lake

When the moon comes out,
let's put the boat in and cast off.
The waves will likely be lapping,
and there will be a little wind.

It may be dark out at sea,
but the water dripping from the oars
will sound intimate
—in the gaps between your words.

The moon will prick up its ears,
maybe descend a little.
When we are to kiss,
it'll hover above our heads.

You will continue talking,
random accounts and daily gripes,
and I will listen to every word,
—but don't stop rowing.

When the moon comes out,
let's put the boat in and cast off.
The waves will likely be lapping,
and there will be a little wind.

湖上

ポッカリ月が出ましたら、
舟を浮べて出掛けませう。
波はヒタヒタ打つでせう、
風も少しはあるでせう。

沖に出たらば暗いでせう、
櫂から滴垂る水の音は
昵懇しいものに聞こえませう、
——あなたの言葉の杜切れ間を。

月は聴き耳立てるでせう、
すこしは降りても来るでせう、
われら接唇する時に
月は頭上にあるでせう。

あなたはなほも、語るでせう、
よしないことや拗言や、
洩らさず私は聴くでせう、
——けれど漕ぐ手はやめないで。

ポッカリ月が出ましたら、
舟を浮べて出掛けませう。
波はヒタヒタ打つでせう、
風も少しはあるでせう。

Winter Night

everyone is quiet tonight
you can hear the kettle
I'm thinking of a woman
although I have no woman

there is no difficulty in
imagining in the incredibly
flexible and air-like realm
I'm drawing a woman

in the incredibly flexible silence
of a perfectly clear night
listening to the sound of the kettle
I'm dreaming of a woman

thus the night deepens
on a winter night when only my dog is awake
shadows and cigarette and me and the dog
that is an indescribable cocktail

冬の夜

みなさん今夜は静かです
薬罐の音がしてゐます
僕は女を想つてる
僕には女がないのです

それで苦労もないのです
えもいはれない弾力の
空気のやうな空想に
女を描いてみてゐるのです

えもいはれない弾力の
澄み亙たる夜の沈黙
薬罐の音を聞きながら
女を夢みてゐるのです

かくて夜は更け夜は深まつて
犬のみ覚めたる冬の夜は
影と煙草と僕と犬
えもいはれないカクテールです

2

nothing better than the air
nothing better than indoor air on a cold night
nothing better than the smoke
nothing more pleasant than the smoke
eventually you will understand
the time will come when you agree with me

nothing better than the air
like a skinny old lady's hand on a chilly night
its flexibility both tender
and tough it has the same flexibility as that hand
like smoke like that woman's passion
as though it burns as though it disappears

nothing is better than indoor air on a winter night

2

空気よりよいものはないのです
それも寒い夜の室内の空気よりもよいものはな
　いのです
煙よりよいものはないのです
煙より　愉快なものもないのです
やがてはそれがお分りなのです
同感なさる時が　来るのです

空気よりよいものはないのです
寒い夜の痩せた年増女の手のやうな
その手の弾力のやうな　やはらかい　またかたい
かたいやうな　その手の弾力のやうな
煙のやうな　その女の情熱のやうな
炎えるやうな　消えるやうな

冬の夜の室内の　空気よりよいものはないのです

Autumn News

This morning, linen clings to people's skin,
and sparrows' voices have grown stiff.
Chimney smoke scatters in the wind.

Dig into the volcanic ash and it's like ice.
A blue sky sinks coldly,
resolutely, into the depths of space.

If you bask on the stone
steps of the church—
flowers dancing in the sun,
and insects rustling in the shade.

Autumn days are warm to the body
but chilly to the hands and feet.
Recently, advertising balloons
arise and drift in the Shinjuku sky.

秋の消息

麻は朝、人の肌に追い縋り
雀らの、声も硬うはなりました
煙突の、煙は風に乱れ散り

火山灰掘れば氷のある如く
けざやけき顥気の底に青空は
冷たく沈み、しみじみと

教会堂の石段に
日向ぼっこをしてあれば
陽光に廻る花々や
物蔭に、すずろすだける虫の音や

秋の日は、からだに暖か
手や足に、ひえびえとして
此の日頃、広告気球は新宿の
空に揚りて漂へり

Bone

Look. This is my bone.
Plagued with hardships while alive,
exposed by rain,
the bone-tip
juts from rotten flesh.

It doesn't shine:
only, with an absurd indifference,
absorbs the rain,
is blown by wind,
reflects the sky a little.

While alive, sometimes it
would sit in a crowded restaurant
or eat boiled honewort
with soy sauce.
How amusing to think of this.

Look. This is my bone—
Aren't I looking at it? How funny.
Does the forsaken spirit
come back to where the bone is
and observe?

In half-withered grass
at the edge of a hometown stream
stands looking—myself?
At just the height of a signpost,
the bone is dissembling, keen.

骨

ホラホラ、これが僕の骨だ、
生きてゐた時の苦労にみちた
あのけがらはしい肉を破つて、
しらじらと雨に洗はれ、
ヌックと出た、骨の尖。

それは光沢もない、
ただいたづらにしらじらと、
雨を吸収する、
風に吹かれる、
幾分空を反映する。

生きてゐた時に、
これが食堂の雑踏の中に、
坐つてゐたこともある、
みつばのおしたしを食つたこともある、
と思へばなんとも可笑しい。

ホラホラ、これが僕の骨——
見てゐるのは僕？　可笑しなことだ。
霊魂はあとに残つて、
また骨の所にやつて来て、
見てゐるのかしら？

故郷の小川のへりに、
半ばは枯れた草に立つて、
見てゐるのは、——僕？
恰度立札ほどの高さに、
骨はしらじらととんがつてゐる。

Autumn Day Madness

I have nothing anymore.
I'm empty-handed
and I don't even lament it.
Finally, I'm without a thing.

Even so, the weather is nice today.
Since a moment ago, many planes are flying.
—Will Europe start a war or not?
Who knows?

The weather is really nice today.
The blue of the sky is wet with tears.
The poplars are fluttering.
The children have already risen to heaven.

No one on the ground but a salaryman's wife
basking in the sun and a shoe repair hawker.
The sound of the hawker's drumbeat
wanders the bright ruins alone, praising them.

Oh, someone come and help me!
In the time of Diogenes, only small birds sang,
but now not even sparrows cry.
Even shadows on the ground look too faint!

秋日狂乱

僕にはもはや何もないのだ
僕は空手空拳だ
おまけにそれを嘆きもしない
僕はいよいよの無一物だ

それにしても今日は好いお天気で
さつきから沢山の飛行機が飛んでゐる
——欧羅巴は戦争を起すのか起さないのか
誰がそんなこと分るものか

今日はほんとに好いお天気で
空の青も涙にうるんでゐる
ポプラがヒラヒラヒラヒラしてゐて
子供等は先刻昇天した

もはや地上には日向ぼつこをしてゐる
月給取の妻君とデーデー屋さん以外にゐない
デーデー屋さんの叩く鼓の音が
明るい廃墟を唯独りで讃美し廻つてゐる

あゝ、誰か来て僕を助けて呉れ
ヂオゲネスの頃には小鳥くらゐ啼いたらうが
けふびは雀も啼いてはをらぬ
地上に落ちた物影でさへ、はや余りに淡い！

—But where has the country girl gone?
Would those pressed purple flowers no longer bleed?
Would the sun no longer shine on the grass?
Isn't there even an illusion of ascent?

What am I saying?
By what confusion am I being swept away?
Where did the butterfly go?
Is it now not spring but autumn?

Ah, well, I'll drink some strong syrup.
I'll drink it cold, through a wide straw.
I'll drink it slowly, never looking away.
I'll ask for nothing, *nothing!* . . .

——さるにても田舎のお嬢さんは何処に去つたか
その紫の押花はもうにじまないのか
草の上には陽は照らぬのか
昇天の幻想だにもはやないのか？

僕は何を云つてゐるのか
如何なる錯乱に掠められてゐるのか
蝶々はどつちへとんでいつたか
今は春でなくて、秋であつたか

ではあゝ、濃いシロップでも飲まう
冷たくして、太いストローで飲まう
とろとろと、脇見もしないで飲まう
何にも、何にも、求めまい！……

Korean Woman

Strands from the Korean woman's clothes
got tangled in the autumn wind.
Up and down the main road
she yanks the child's hand
with unnecessary force.
That face, with its dry, coppery red skin,
what is it thinking?
—Truly, I'm also miserable,
my mind lost in a daze.

You eyed me with suspicion
and hurried your child away . . .
The light dust that has risen,
what does it want me to think?
The light dust that has risen,
what does it want me to think? . . .
. . . .

朝鮮女

朝鮮女の服の紐
秋の風に縒れたらん
街道を往くをりをりは
子供の手をば無理に引き
額顰めし汝が面ぞ
肌赤銅の乾物にて
なにを思へるその顔ぞ
——まことやわれもうらぶれし
こころに呆け見ゐたりけむ

われを打見ていぶかりて
子供うながし去りゆけり……
軽く立ちたる埃かも
何をかわれに思へとや
軽く立ちたる埃かも
何をかわれに思へとや……
. . . .

A Dream I Awoke to On a Summer Night

When I closed my eyes to sleep,
all I could see on the pitch black field
were the faint white uniforms of the nine
baseball players I had seen that day—

Each of the nine was in his defensive position.
The sly pitcher was the same as always,
and the joker of a second baseman
in high spirits as usual.

Well, the hit I was waiting for didn't come,
and just as I was thinking, "Oh well,"
the nine plus the batters all disappeared,
and not a soul was left on the field.

Soon it was a hot midday on the field.
The surrounding poplar trees
were green and fluttered their leaves.
The buzz of cicadas continued for a while.
And as I was thinking, "Oh well . . . " I drifted off.

夏の夜に覚めてみた夢

眠らうとして目をば閉ぢると
真ッ暗なグランドの上に
その日昼みた野球のナインの
ユニホームばかりほのかに白く——

ナインは各々守備位置にあり
狡さうなピッチャは相も変らず
お調子者のセカンドは
相も変らぬお調子ぶりの

扨、待つてゐるヒットは出なく
やれやれと思つてゐると
ナインも打者も悉く消え
人ッ子一人ゐはしないグランドは

忽ち暑い真昼のグランド
グランド繞るポプラ竝木は
蒼々として葉をひるがへし
ひときはつづく蝉しぐれ
やれやれと思つてゐるうち……眠た

Spring and Baby

Sleeping in a field of rapeflower . . .
in a field of rapeflower blown about by the wind . . .
is that a baby?

No. Creaking in the sky are lines—the power lines.
All day those power lines creak in the sky.
But crying in the field of rapeflower—that is a baby.

What runs past is a bike bike bike,
running along the far side path
with the pale pink wind at its back . . .

With the pale pink wind at their back
run the rapeflowers and white clouds in the sky
—leaving the baby behind in the field.

春と赤ン坊

菜の花畑で眠つてゐるのは……
菜の花畑で吹かれてゐるのは……
赤ン坊ではないでせうか？

いいえ、空で鳴るのは、電線です電線です
ひねもす、空で鳴るのは、あれは電線です
菜の花畑に眠つてゐるのは、赤ン坊ですけど

走つてゆくのは、自転車々々々
向ふの道を、走つてゆくのは
薄桃色の、風を切つて……

薄桃色の、風を切つて
走つてゆくのは菜の花畑や空の白雲
——赤ン坊を畑に置いて

Skylarks

all day against the sky they creak
ah the lines the power lines
all day against the sky they cry
ah children of the clouds skylarks

in the blue blue sky
they wheel around and around
crying *pi—chiku-chiku*
ah cloud children the skylarks

I walk across a field of rapeflower
toward the horizon to the horizon
I walk through these mountains
under the blue the blue sky

sleeping in a field of rapeflower
in a rapeflower field asleep
among rapeflowers blown by the wind
sleeping there is that a baby?

雲雀

ひねもす空で鳴りますは
あゝ　電線だ、電線だ
ひねもす空で啼きますは
あゝ　雲の子だ、雲雀奴だ

碧い　碧い空の中
ぐるぐるぐると　潜りこみ
ピーチクチクと啼きますは
あゝ　雲の子だ、雲雀奴だ

歩いてゆくのは菜の花畑
地平の方へ、地平の方へ
歩いてゆくのはあの山この山
あーをい　あーをい空の下

眠つてゐるのは、菜の花畑に
菜の花畑に、眠つてゐるのは
菜の花畑で風に吹かれて
眠つてゐるのは赤ン坊だ？

Early Summer Night

Summer has come again,
and at night a polar bear made of steam
comes across the marsh.
—Many things have happened.
I've done a lot of different things.
Yes, there were happy moments,
but when I think back, it all becomes sad.
Like the sound of creaking iron,
as the presence of dusk comes over them,
infants, elderly, the youth and adults alike
together let out such lovely voices,
and beneath the moths fluttering in the twilight,
their jaws are delicate, lovely.
So, although tonight is a fine June night,
and distant sounds are carried pleasantly on the wind,
I feel a certain sadness
at the echo of the iron bridge that just vanished.
Above that bridge over the great river, the sky is slate gray.

初夏の夜

また今年も夏が来て、
夜は、蒸気で出来た白熊が、
沼をわたつてやつてくる。
——色々のことがあつたんです。
色々のことをして来たものです。
嬉しいことも、あつたのですが、
回想されては、すべてがかなしい
鉄製の、軋音さながら
なべては夕暮迫るけはひに
幼年も、老年も、青年も壮年も、
共々に余りに可憐な声をばあげて、
薄暮の中で舞ふ蛾の下で
はかなくも可憐な顎をしてゐるのです。
されば今夜六月の良夜なりとはいへ、
遠いい物音が、心地よく風に送られて来るとはいへ、
なにがなし悲しい思ひであるのは、
消えたばかしの鉄橋の響音
大河の、その鉄橋の上方に、空はぼんやりと石盤色であるのです。

Northern Sea

In the sea,
that is no mermaid.
In the sea,
those are only waves.

Under a cloudy north sea sky
waves snarl here and there.
They are cursing the sky.
A curse that may never end.

In the sea,
that is no mermaid.
In the sea,
those are only waves.

北の海

海にゐるのは、
あれは人魚ではないのです。
海にゐるのは、
あれは、浪ばかり。

曇つた北海の空の下、
浪はところどころ歯をむいて、
空を呪ろつてゐるのです。
いつはてるとも知れない呪。

海にゐるのは、
あれは人魚ではないのです。
海にゐるのは、
あれは、浪ばかり。

Song of Innocence

When I think about it, I've come a long way.
Where now is the whistle steam
that rang in the harbor sky
that winter night when I was twelve?

The moon was among the clouds,
and when it heard that whistle,
it froze up in shock
and the moon was in that time and space.

How many years have passed since then?
Where now is that me who
in a daze followed the whistle
steam with his eyes and grew sad?

Now that I have a wife and child,
I think I've come a long way.
Even so, I wonder
if I'm going to live much longer.

Even if I live a while longer,
I'll miss those long ago
days and nights so much now
that I can't really be confident.

And yet, as long as I do live,
in the end I will always be diligent,
which is kind of pitiful,
if I do say so myself.

頑是ない歌

思へば遠く来たもんだ
十二の冬のあの夕べ
港の空に鳴り響いた
汽笛の湯気げは今いづこ

雲の間に月はゐて
それな汽笛を耳にすると
竦然として身をすくめ
月はその時空にゐた

それから何年経つたことか
汽笛の湯気を茫然と
眼で追ひかなしくなつてゐた
あの頃の俺はいまいづこ

今では女房子供持ち
思へば遠く来たもんだ
此の先まだまだ何時までか
生きてゆくのであらうけど

生きてゆくのであらうけど
遠く経て来た日や夜の
あんまりこんなにこひしゆては
なんだか自信が持てないよ

さりとて生きてゆく限り
結局我ン張る僕の性質
と思へばなんだか我ながら
いたはしいよなものですよ

If you think about it,
it's mere diligence after all,
but sometimes I miss the old days.
I'll just have to muddle through.

Simple when you think about it.
All a matter of willpower.
No choice but to do something.
All you have to do is do it.

That's what I think, but there it is.
Oh, where now is the whistle steam
that rang in the harbor sky
that winter night when I was twelve?

考へてみればそれはまあ
結局我ン張るのだとして
昔恋しい時もあり　そして
どうにかやつてはゆくのでせう

考へてみれば簡単だ
畢竟意志の問題だ
なんとかやるより仕方もない
やりさへすればよいのだと

思ふけれどもそれもそれ
十二の冬のあの夕べ
港の空に鳴り響いた
汽笛の湯気や今いづこ

Quiet

With nothing to consider,
my heart is quiet.

It's a breezeway Sunday—
everyone has gone to the fields.

The boards have a cool luster,
and little birds are singing in the garden.

From a faucet left dripping,
droplets gleam brightly!

Soil a rosy color, larks in the sky,
a sky that's lovely in April.

With nothing to consider,
my heart is quiet.

閑寂

なんにも訪ふことのない、
私の心は閑寂だ。

　　――それは日曜日の渡り廊下、
　　みんなは野原へ行つちやつた。

板は冷たい光沢をもち、
小鳥は庭に啼いてゐる。

　　締めの足りない水道の、
　　蛇口の滴は、つと光り！

土は薔薇色、空には雲雀
空はきれいな四月です。

　　なんにも訪ふことのない、
　　私の心は閑寂だ。

Clown Song

Who taught the blind girl
about moonlight?
Was it Beethoven or Schubert?
The image in my memory
is a bit broken tonight,
but I think it was Tovy,
although maybe it was Berty?

On a foggy autumn night,
seated on the stone garden steps
and basking in the moonlight,
the two of them were silent for a while,
but then went in to the piano room
and played almost to the point of tears.
That was—wasn't that Berty?

お道化うた

月の光のそのことを、
盲目少女に教へたは、
ベートーヹンか、シューバート？
俺の記憶の錯覚が、
今夜とちれてゐるけれど、
ベトちやんだとは思ふけど、
シュバちやんではなかつたらうか？

霧の降つたる秋の夜に、
庭・石段に腰掛けて、
月の光を浴びながら、
二人、黙つてゐたけれど、
やがてピアノの部屋に入り、
泣かんばかりに弾き出した、
あれは、シュバちやんではなかつたらうか？

Looking at the dim city lights,
on the outskirts of Vienna,
on a night when stars seemed to be falling,
with insects swarming in the grass,
the teacher's thirteenth son
that man with a short neck, who,
as if taking the blind girl's hand,
slumped over the piano,
with his sweaty forehead
and dirt-cheap glasses,
the swayback who played so pitifully,
like he was coughing it up,
That was—wasn't that Berty?

Berty or Tovy,
I don't know about that,
but on this starry Tokyo night,
if I tilt my beer cup
and look at the moonlight,

Tovy and Berty both died young.
They both died young,
and there's no reason for anyone to know . . .

かすむ街の灯とほに見て、
ウキンの市の郊外に、
星も降るよなその夜さ一と夜、
虫、草叢にすだく頃、
教師の息子の十三番目、
頸の短いあの男、
盲目少女の手をとるやうに、
ピアノの上に勢ひ込んだ、
汗の出さうなその額、
安物くさいその眼鏡、
丸い背中もいぢらしく
吐き出すやうに弾いたのは、
あれは、シュバちやんではなかつたらうか？

シュバちやんかベトちやんか、
そんなこと、いざ知らね、
今宵星降る東京の夜、
ビールのコップを傾けて、
月の光を見てあれば、

ベトちやんもシュバちやんも、はやとほに死に、
はやとほに死んだことさへ、
誰知らうことわりもない……

Memory

On a fine day, the offshore waves—
my, how beautiful they are!
On a fine day, aren't the offshore waves
like gold and silver?

I was drawn to the edge of the cape
by the gold and silver waves,
but the gold and silver
just kept shining brightly offshore.

At the edge of the cape was a brickyard,
and bricks were drying in the yard.
The drying bricks shone brightly,
yet the factory was silent.

I took a seat in the brickyard
and smoked for a while.
As I was smoking, in a daze
I heard the waves rumbling offshore.

As the offshore waves rumbled,
I sat there idly, in a daze.
Sitting there in a daze, my head
and chest got nice and warm.

思ひ出

お天気の日の、海の沖は
なんと、あんなに綺麗なんだ！
お天気の日の、海の沖は、
まるで、金や、銀ではないか

金や銀の沖の波に、
ひかれひかれて、岬の端に
やつて来たれど金や銀は
なほもとほのき、沖で光つた。

岬の端には煉瓦工場が、
工場の庭には煉瓦干されて、
煉瓦干されて赫々してゐた
しかも工場は、音とてなかつた

煉瓦工場に、腰をば据ゑて、
私は暫く煙草を吹かした。
煙草吹かしてぼんやりしてると、
沖の方では波が鳴つてた。

沖の方では波が鳴らうと、
私はかまはずぼんやりしてゐた。
ぼんやりしてると頭も胸も
ポカポカポカポカ暖かだつた

It was really nice and warm.
The brickyard on the cape was struck by spring sun.
The brickyard made no sound.
Birds were singing in the grove behind it.

Although the birds were singing, the brickyard
stood unshakable, stock still.
Although the birds were singing, the brickyard
windows were struck by sunlight.

Although the window panes were struck by sunlight,
they didn't seem warm at all.
A brickyard at the edge of the cape
on a fine day in early spring!

*

The brickyard later fell into disuse.
The brickyard died.
The brickyard windows and glass
now lie in ruins.

The brickyard is desolate and haggard.
It still stands idly before the grove.
Although birds still sing in the grove,
the brickyard is just decaying.

ポカポカポカポカ暖かだつたよ
岬の工場は春の陽をうけ、
煉瓦工場は音とてもなく
裏の木立で鳥が啼いてた

鳥が啼いても煉瓦工場は、
ビクともしないでジッとしてゐた
鳥が啼いても煉瓦工場の、
窓の硝子は陽をうけてゐた

窓の硝子は陽をうけてても
ちつとも暖かさうではなかつた
春のはじめのお天気の日の
岬の端の煉瓦工場よ！

＊

煉瓦工場は、その後廃れて、
煉瓦工場は、死んでしまつた
煉瓦工場の、窓も硝子も、
今は毀れてゐようといふもの

煉瓦工場は、廃れて枯れて、
木立の前に、今もぼんやり
木立に鳥は、今も啼くけど
煉瓦工場は、朽ちてゆくだけ

Offshore waves still rumble
and sun shines on garden soil,
but workmen don't come to the brickyard,
and I don't go to the brickyard either.

The chimney that once blew smoke
now just stands there, looking eerie.
On rainy days, it's especially eerie.
Even on sunny days, it's kind of eerie.

Even though it used to look kind of eerie,
the chimney can do nothing now.
Sometimes this great veteran
has frightening eyes filled with hate.

Those eyes are so frightening that today
again I came out to the beach, sat on a rock
and looked down in a daze.
My chest even began to pound.

沖の波は、今も鳴るけど
庭の土には、陽が照るけれど
煉瓦工場に、人夫は来ない
煉瓦工場に、僕も行かない

嘗て煙を、吐いてた煙突も、
今はぶきみに、たゞ立つてゐる
雨の降る日は、殊にもぶきみ
晴れた日だとて、相当ぶきみ

相当ぶきみな、煙突でさへ
今ぢやどうさへ、手出しも出来ず
この尨大な、古強者が
時々恨む、その眼は怖い

その眼は怖くて、今日も僕は
浜へ出て来て、石に腰掛け
ぼんやり俯き、案じてゐれば
僕の胸さへ、波を打つのだ

Late Summer Heat

Let's lie down on the tatami mats
with the flies buzzing around us.
Someone said this morning that
even the tatami has turned yellow.

As I rambled on about this and that,
memories came to mind.
While they were floating around,
before I knew it, I'd dozed off.

When I awoke, it was nearly dusk.
And although birds were still singing,
the treetops bathed in sun,
I watered the garden trees.

Water on leaf ends of the low branches of the trees.
I watched it glisten forever in the light.

残暑

畳の上に、寝ころばう、
蝿はブンブン　唸つてる
畳ももはや　黄色くなつたと
今朝がた　誰かが云つてゐたつけ

それやこれやと　とりとめもなく
僕の頭に　記憶は浮かび
浮かぶがまゝに　浮かべてゐるうち
いつしか　僕は眠つてゐたのだ

覚めたのは　夕方ちかく
まだかなかなは　啼いてたけれど
樹々の梢は　陽を受けてたけど、
僕は庭木に　打水やつた

　　打水が、樹々の下枝の葉の尖に
　　光つてゐるのをいつまでも、
　　　僕は見てゐた

New Year's Eve Bell

The New Year's Eve bell rings in the dark, distant sky.
Trembling the stale night air for ten million years,
the New Year's Eve bell rings in the dark, distant sky.

It is the foggy haze of a temple forest . . .
That is where it rings and from where it resonates.
It is the foggy haze of a temple forest . . .

In those days, children would eat soba at their parents' knees.
In those days, Ginza was packed, Asakusa also packed with people.
In those days, children would eat soba at their parents' knees.

In those days, Ginza was teeming, and Asakusa also teeming with people.
In those days, I wonder how prisoners felt. How did they feel?
In those days, Ginza was teeming, and Asakusa also teeming with people.

The New Year's Eve bell rings in the dark, distant sky.
Trembling the stale night air for ten million years,
the New Year's Eve bell rings in the dark, distant sky.

除夜の鐘

除夜の鐘は暗い遠いい空で鳴る。
千万年も、古びた夜の空気を顫はし、
除夜の鐘は暗い遠いい空で鳴る。

それは寺院の森の霧つた空……
そのあたりで鳴つて、そしてそこから響いて来る。
それは寺院の森の霧つた空……

その時子供は父母の膝下で蕎麦を食うべ、
その時銀座はいつぱいの人出、浅草もいつぱいの人出、
その時子供は父母の膝下で蕎麦を食うべ。

その時銀座はいつぱいの人出、浅草もいつぱいの人出。
その時囚人は、どんな心持だらう、どんな心持だらう、
その時銀座はいつぱいの人出、浅草もいつぱいの人出。

除夜の鐘は暗い遠いい空で鳴る。
千万年も、古びた夜の空気を顫はし、
除夜の鐘は暗い遠いい空で鳴る。

Ode to Snow

When it snows, life is
a sad yet beautiful thing—
full of melancholy, or so it seems to me.

That snow fell on the walls of dark medieval castles,
and also in the time of Gengo Ōtaka . . .

Many an orphan's hands
went numb because of it,
and evenings in the city were sad enough.

Snow seen beyond the fences
of Russian vacation homes
is wearyingly eternal,

and on snowy days, even a noblewoman
might complain a bit, I reckon . . .

When it snows, life is
a sad yet beautiful thing—
full of melancholy, or so it seems to me.

雪の賦

雪が降るとこのわたくしには、人生が、
かなしくもうつくしいものに――
憂愁にみちたものに、思へるのであつた。

その雪は、中世の、暗いお城の塀にも降り、
大高源吾の頃にも降つた……

幾多々々の孤児の手は、
そのためにかじかんで、
都会の夕べはそのために十分悲しくあつたのだ。

ロシアの田舎の別荘の、
矢来の彼方に見る雪は、
うんざりする程永遠で、

雪の降る日は高貴の夫人も、
ちつとは愚痴でもあらうと思はれ……

雪が降るとこのわたくしには、人生が
かなしくもうつくしいものに――
憂愁にみちたものに、思へるのであつた。

My Half Life

I've suffered many hardships.
As for what those hardships were,
I have no desire to talk about it.
Nor have I given any thought
as to whether those hardships
were worth it or not.

Anyway, I've suffered hardships.
Have suffered hardships!
And so now I find myself here,
sitting before my desk.
All I can do is to
hold out my hand and stare at it.

Outside tonight, tree leaves rustle.
Spring evening with a distant feel to it.
And I will die quietly,
just sit here and die.

わが半生

私は随分苦労して来た。
それがどうした苦労であつたか、
語らうなぞとはつゆさへ思はぬ。
またその苦労が果して価値の
あつたものかなかつたものか、
そんなことなぞ考へてもみぬ。

とにかく私は苦労して来た。
苦労して来たことであつた！
そして、今、此処、机の前の、
自分を見出すばつかりだ。
じつと手を出し眺めるほどの
ことしか私は出来ないのだ。

　外では今宵、木の葉がそよぐ。
　はるかな気持の、春の宵だ。
　そして私は、静かに死ぬる、
　坐つたまんまで、死んでゆくのだ。

Single

Autumn wind blew on a soapbox.
Along the road that separates the suburbs from the city,
a woman from Ohara was walking alone.

—He was single.
He was terribly myopic.
He usually wore formal attire.
He had once worked as a hanko shop apprentice.

He had just left a bathhouse.
At three in the afternoon under faint sunlight,
wind blew on a soapbox.
Along the road that separates the suburbs from the city,
a woman from Ohara was walking alone.

hanko: a signature stamp. The shops that made them also lent money and were a staple of the Shōwa working class.

独身者

石鹸箱には秋風が吹き
郊外と、市街を限る路の上には
大原女が一人歩いてゐた

——彼は独身者であつた
彼は極度の近眼であつた
彼はよそゆきを普段に着てゐた
判屋奉公したこともあつた

今しも彼が湯屋から出て来る
薄日の射してる午後の三時
石鹸箱には風が吹き
郊外と、市街を限る路の上には
大原女が一人歩いてゐた

Spring Evening Nostalgia

The rain has stopped. Wind blows.
  Passing clouds obscure the moon.
Tonight's a spring night, everyone.
  A lukewarm wind blows.

Somehow, a deep sigh,
  some kind of vague fantasy,
arises, but I can't grasp it.
  Can't tell anyone about it.

It's something that can't be
  spoken about with anyone,
but isn't that life?
  And yet, I can't show it . . .

Every human being feels this way
  in their heart, and whenever
we meet, we just crack a smile,
  and so our lives pass by.

The rain has stopped. Wind blows.
  Clouds flow, obscure the moon.
Tonight's a spring night, everyone.
  A lukewarm wind blows.

春宵感懐

雨が、あがつて、風が吹く。
　雲が、流れる、月かくす。
みなさん、今夜は、春の宵。
　なまあつたかい、風が吹く。

なんだか、深い、溜息が、
　なんだかはるかな、幻想が、
湧くけど、それは、摑めない。
　誰にも、それは、語れない。

誰にも、それは、語れない
　ことだけれども、それこそが、
いのちだらうぢやないですか、
　けれども、それは、示かせない……

かくて、人間、ひとりびとり、
　こころで感じて、顔見合せれば
につこり笑ふといふほどの
　ことして、一生、過ぎるんですねえ

雨が、あがつて、風が吹く。
　雲が、流れる、月かくす。
みなさん、今夜は、春の宵。
　なまあつたかい、風が吹く。

Cloudy Sky

One morning, up in the sky,
I saw a fluttering black flag.
It fluttered in the wind,
but so high I couldn't hear the sound.

I tried to reel it down, but since
that couldn't happen without a rope,
the flag continued to flutter,
dancing into the depths of the sky.

I think of how often I saw the like
on mornings of my youth.
Then, I watched them from a field.
Now it's from a city rooftop.

Then and now, the times divide.
Places differ, here and there.
Still fluttering alone in the sky,
that immutable black flag.

曇天

　ある朝　僕は　空の　中に、
黒い　旗が　はためくを　見た。
　はたはた　それは　はためいて　ゐたが、
音は　きこえぬ　高きが　ゆゑに。

　手繰り　下ろさうと　僕は　したが、
綱も　なければ　それも　叶はず、
　旗は　はたはた　はためく　ばかり、
空の　奥処に　舞ひ入る　如く。

　かゝる　朝を　少年の　日も、
屢々　見たりと　僕は　憶ふ。
　かの時は　そを　野原の　上に、
今はた　都会の　甍の　上に。

　かの時　この時　時は　隔つれ、
此処と　彼処と　所は　異れ、
　はたはた　はたはた　み空に　ひとり、
いまも　渝らぬ　かの　黒旗よ。

To the Dragonflies

a sky too bright   for autumn
red dragonflies   are flying
I stand   in a field
lazing   in the pale sunset

faraway factory   chimneys appear
hazy   in the setting sun
I let out   a deep sigh
kneel down   and pick up a stone

after a while   the cold stone
begins to warm   in my hand
I toss it aside   pull up some grass
pull up grass   lazing in the sunset

the pulled grass   withers ever
so slowly   on the soil
faraway factory   chimneys appear
hazy   in the setting sun

蜻蛉に寄す

あんまり晴れてる　秋の空
赤い蜻蛉が　飛んでゐる
淡い夕陽を　浴びながら
僕は野原に　立つてゐる

遠くに工場の　煙突が
夕陽にかすんで　みえてゐる
大きな溜息　一つついて
僕は蹲んで　石を拾ふ

その石くれの　冷たさが
漸く手中で　ぬくもると
僕は放して　今度は草を
夕陽を浴びてる　草を抜く

抜かれた草は　土の上で
ほのかほのかに　萎えてゆく
遠くに工場の　煙突は
夕陽に霞んで　みえてゐる

AUTUMN OF ETERNAL FAREWELL

永訣の秋

I Will Never Return

—Kyoto—

I was at the edge of the world. The sun was shining warmly and a breeze was rustling the flowers.

Dust on the wooden bridge was silent all day, the postbox shone brightly all day, and a stroller with a pinwheel attached to it was always parked in town.

None of the people or children who lived there could be seen on the streets, and I had no relatives. My job was to occasionally look at the color of the sky above the weathervane.

But it wasn't boring. Nectar was in the air, and this nectar, being incorporeal, was suitable for daily consumption.

I tried smoking cigarettes, but only liked the smell. What's more, I only smoked outside.

Now, my only prized possession was a single towel. Although I had a pillow, there was no hope of a futon. At least I had a toothbrush, but my one book had nothing written inside; I would pick it up periodically and just enjoy its weight.

ゆきてかへらぬ

——京都——

僕は此の世の果てにゐた。陽は温暖に降り洒ぎ、風は花々揺つてゐた。

木橋の、埃りは終日、沈黙し、ポストは終日赫々と、風車を付けた乳母車、いつも街上に停つてゐた。

棲む人達は子供等は、街上に見えず、僕に一人の縁者なく、風信機の上の空の色、時々見るのが仕事であつた。

さりとて退屈してもゐず、空気の中には蜜があり、物体ではないその蜜は、常住食すに適してゐた。

煙草くらゐは喫つてもみたが、それとて匂ひを好んだばかり。おまけに僕としたことが、戸外でしか吹かさなかつた。

さてわが親しき所有品は、タオル一本。枕は持つてゐたとはいへ、布団ときたらば影だになく、歯刷子くらゐは持つてもゐたが、たつた一冊ある本は、中に何も書いてはなく、時々手にとりその目方、たのしむだけのものだつた。

I was deeply in love with the women, but never once thought of going to visit them. I just dreamed about them a lot.

Something indescribable kept urging me on, and although I had no goal, hope was pounding in my chest.

*

In the middle of the forest was a mysterious park where eerily smiling women, children and men were strolling around, talking to me in a language I didn't understand, expressing emotions I didn't understand.

Now, in that sky, spider webs were shining with a silver light.

女たちは、げに慕はしいのではあつたが、一度とて、会ひに行かうと思はなかつた。夢みるだけで沢山だつた。

名状しがたい何物かゞ、たえず僕をば促進し、目的もない僕ながら、希望は胸に高鳴つてゐた。

*

林の中には、世にも不思議な公園があつて、無気味な程にもにこやかな、女や子供、男達散歩してゐて、僕に分らぬ言語を話し、僕に分らぬ感情を、表情してゐた。

さてその空には銀色に、蜘蛛の巣が光り輝いてゐた。

A Fairy Tale

One autumn night, in a place far away,
there was a dry riverbed of pebbles,
and the sunlight, *sarasara*,
sarasara, was filtering down upon it.

But the sunlight was something like silica
or an unearthly fine powder,
which is why *sarasara*
was also the faint sound it made.

Now, a butterfly lighted on one of the pebbles.
It cast a shadow
sharp and colorless.

The butterfly soon faded away. And then,
along the riverbed where never had it flowed before,
water was suddenly babbling, *sarasara, sarasara* . . .

sarasara: onomatopoeia that expresses a light, repeated sound, often of wind or water

一つのメルヘン

秋の夜は、はるかの彼方に、
小石ばかりの、河原があつて、
それに陽は、さらさらと
さらさらと射してゐるのでありました。

陽といつても、まるで珪石か何かのやうで、
非常な個体の粉末のやうで、
さればこそ、さらさらと
かすかな音を立ててもゐるのでした。

さて小石の上に、今しも一つの蝶がとまり、
淡い、それでゐてくつきりとした
影を落としてゐるのでした。

やがてその蝶がみえなくなると、いつのまにか、
今迄流れてもゐなかつた川床に、水は
さらさらと、さらさらと流れてゐるので
　ありました……

Illusion

At some point, a transient, unfortunate
clown lived alone in my head.
He wore a gauzy outfit
and would bask in the moonlight.

Sometimes he would make a weak hand gesture.
He was constantly making hand gestures,
but the meaning never came through,
which just made me pity him.

He was making hand gestures and moving his lips,
but it was like watching an old shadow puppet—
there wasn't the slightest sound,
nor could I understand what he was saying.

With moonlight bathing his body in white,
in a strange and bright mist
he gently moved his faint figure,
and his eyes were filled with an endless warmth.

幻影

私の頭の中には、いつの頃からか、
薄命さうなピエロがひとり棲んでゐて、
それは、紗の服なんかを着込んで、
そして、月光を浴びてゐるのでした。

ともすると、弱々しげな手付をして、
しきりと　手真似をするのでしたが、
その意味が、つひぞ通じたためしはなく、
あわれげな　思ひをさせるばつかりでした。

手真似につれては、唇も動かしてゐるのでしたが、
古い影絵でも見てゐるやう——
音はちつともしないのですし、
何を云つてるのかは　分りませんでした。

しろじろと身に月光を浴び、
あやしくもあかるい霧の中で、
かすかな姿態をゆるやかに動かしながら、
眼付きばかりはどこまでも、やさしさうなのでした。

The Slut's Husband Sang

You love me.
You have never hated me.

I love you, too.
Seems it was decided in a past life.

And our two souls love each other in ignorance and calm,
a habit of many years.

And yet, within us both lie
terribly unfaithful hearts,

and we sometimes find the most natural
feelings of love tiresome.

More than the scent of fine perfume,
we long for the faint smell of the hospital.

There, the two closest people
sometimes hate each other the most.

And afterwards we're overcome
with a sublime sense of regret.

Ah, there's fickleness in us both,
and it blinds us to the truth.

More than the scent of fine perfume,
we long for the faint smell of the hospital.

あばずれ女の亭主が歌つた

おまへはおれを愛してる、一度とて
おれを憎んだためしはない。

おれもおまへを愛してる。前世から
さだまつていることのやう。

そして二人の魂は、不識に温和に愛し合ふ
もう長年の習慣だ。

それなのにまた二人には、
ひどく浮気な心があつて、

いちばん自然な愛の気持を、
時にうるさく思ふのだ。

佳い香水のかをりより、
病院の、あはい匂ひに慕ひよる。

そこでいちばん親しい二人が、
時にいちばん憎みあふ。

そしてあとでは得態の知れない
悔の気持に浸るのだ。

あゝ、二人には浮気があつて、
それが真実を見えなくしちまふ。

佳い香水のかをりより、
病院の、あはい匂ひに慕ひよる。

Song Without Words

it's really far off
but I should wait here
here the air is faint and dull green
as pale as the roots of a spring onion

I shouldn't be in a rush
should wait here a long time
shouldn't gaze into the distance with virginal eyes
surely I should just wait here

even so it was far away and hazy in the dusk
thick and delicate like the sound of a whistle
but I shouldn't run off in that direction
surely I have to wait here

if I do my panting will settle down
and I can surely get that far
however like chimney smoke
it kept drifting   forever in the crimson sky

言葉なき歌

あれはとほいい処にあるのだけれど
おれは此処で待つてゐなくてはならない。
此処は空気もかすかで蒼く
葱の根のやうに仄かに淡い

決して急いではならない
此処で十分待つてゐなければならない
処女の眼のやうに遥かを見遣つてはならない
たしかに此処で待つてゐればよい

それにしてもあれはとほいい彼方で夕陽にけぶ
　つてゐた
号笛の音のやうに太くて繊弱だつた
けれどもその方へ駆け出してはならない
たしかに此処で待つてゐなければならない

さうすればそのうち喘ぎも平静に復し
たしかにあすこまでゆけるに違ひない
しかしあれは煙突の煙のやうに
とほくとほく　いつまでも茜の空にたなびいてゐた

Moonlit Beach

One moonlit night, I found
a single button on the shore.

I picked it up without a thought
to use it for anything, but
somehow couldn't bear to throw it away,
so I tucked it in my sleeve.

One moonlit night, I found
a single button on the shore.

I picked it up without a thought
to use it for anything, but
        could not throw it to the moon,
        nor could I throw it to the waves,
so I tucked it in my sleeve.

The single button I picked up on a moonlit night
stung my fingers, stung my heart.

The single button I picked up on a moonlit night—
how could one throw it away?

月夜の浜辺

月夜の晩に、ボタンが一つ
波打際に、落ちてゐた。

それを拾つて、役立てようと
僕は思つたわけでもないが
なぜだかそれを捨てるに忍びず
僕はそれを、袂に入れた。

月夜の晩に、ボタンが一つ
波打際に、落ちてゐた。

それを拾つて、役立てようと
僕は思つたわけでもないが
　　月に向つてそれは抛れず
　　浪に向つてそれは抛れず
僕はそれを、袂に入れた。

月夜の晩に、拾つたボタンは
指先に沁み、心に沁みた。

月夜の晩に、拾つたボタンは
どうしてそれが、捨てられようか？

Spring Will Come Again

People say spring will come again,
but for me that means pain.
What will happen when spring comes?
The child will not come back.

I think of last May, when I held
you in my arms at the zoo.
Even when I showed you the elephant—
even the birds you called "kitty."

When at last I showed you the deer,
only then did you say nothing. Just stared.
Surely fascinated by its antlers.

You were at that time
in the midst of all the world's light,
manifesting the karma of your gaze . . .

また来ん春……

また来ん春と人は云ふ
しかし私は辛いのだ
春が来たつて何になろ
あの子が返つて来るぢやない

おもへば今年の五月には
おまへを抱いて動物園
象を見せても猫といひ
鳥を見せても猫だつた

最後に見せた鹿だけは
角によつぽど惹かれてか
何とも云はず　眺めてた

ほんにおまへもあの時は
此の世の光のたゞ中に
立つて眺めてゐたつけが……

Moonlight – I

moonlight was shining
moonlight was shining

in a grassy corner of the garden
what's hiding is a dead child

moonlight was shining
moonlight was shining

oh Tircis and Aminte
are coming out on the lawn

they brought a guitar
but just left it somewhere

moonlight was shining
moonlight was shining

月の光　その一

月の光が照つてゐた
月の光が照つてゐた

　　お庭の隅の草叢に
　　隠れてゐるのは死んだ児だ

月の光が照つてゐた
月の光が照つてゐた

　　おや、チルシスとアマントが
　　芝生の上に出て来てる

ギタアを持つては来てゐるが
おつぽり出してあるばかり

　　月の光が照つてゐた
　　月の光が照つてゐた

Moonlight – II

oh Tircis and Aminte
are coming out to play in the garden

tonight is such a spring night
there is also a humid mist

shining in moonlight
on the garden bench

they have a guitar nearby
but seem like they'll never strum it

beyond the lawn is a forest
that is completely dark

oh while Tircis and Aminte
whisper to each other

the dead child is crouching
like a firefly in the forest

月の光　その二

おゝチルシスとアマントが
庭に出て来て遊んでる

ほんに今夜は春の宵
なまあつたかい靄もある

月の光に照らされて
庭のベンチの上にゐる

ギタアがそばにはあるけれど
いつかう弾き出しさうもない

芝生のむかふは森でして
とても黒々してゐます

おゝチルシスとアマントが
こそこそ話してゐる間

森の中では死んだ子が
蛍のやうに蹲んでる

The Village Clock

the big village clock
ticked all day long

the paint on the face
had lost its luster

upon closer inspection
many small cracks could be seen

even in the setting sun
it had a quiet color

before striking the hour
it wheezed

whether it was the face or the gears that made the noise
neither I nor anyone knew

村の時計

村の大きな時計は、
ひねもす動いてゐた

その字板のペンキは
もう艶が消えてゐた

近寄つてみると、
小さなひびが沢山にあるのだつた

それで夕陽が当つてさへが、
おとなしい色をしてゐた

時を打つ前には、
ぜいぜいと鳴つた

字板が鳴るのか中の機械が鳴るのか
僕にも誰にも分らなかつた

Portrait of a Certain Man

1

This sophisticated man who had come back from the West
kept wearing green oil in his hair, even when he got older.

Appearing at the café every night
to chat with the boss, he was a sad sight.

I felt such pity upon hearing he had died.

在る男の肖像

1

洋行帰りのその洒落者は、
齢をとつても髪に緑の油をつけてた。

夜毎喫茶店にあらはれて、
其処の主人と話してゐる様はあはれげであつた。

死んだと聞いてはいつそうあはれであつた。

2

—Disenchantment is the color of steel.

He went out through an open door
into a twilight garden
of lustrous hair and golden lamps.

His freshly shaven neck, his wrists
and everywhere else
felt cold.

Through the open doorway,
regret was blowing in
as relentlessly as the wind.

Reading, passionate love
and hot tea were swept away
in the twilight sky and the wind.

3

She
crawled into the wall.
So, he was alone,
wiping the table in his room.

2

——幻滅は鋼のいろ。

髪毛の艶と、ラムプの金との夕まぐれ
庭に向つて、開け放たれた戸口から、
彼は戸外に出て行つた。

剃りたての、頚条も手頚も
どこもかしこもそはそはと、
寒かつた。

開け放たれた戸口から
悔恨は、風と一緒に容赦なく
吹込んでゐた。

読書も、しむみりした恋も、
暖かいお茶も黄昏の空とともに
風とともにもう其処にはなかつた。

3

彼女は
壁の中へ這入つてしまつた。
それで彼は独り、
部屋で卓子を拭いてゐた。

Chōmon Gorge in Winter

Water was flowing in Chōmon Gorge.
It was turning into an icy cold day.

I was in a fine restaurant.
Pouring myself a drink.

There were no other customers
besides me.

The water flowed and flowed
like something that had a soul.

After a time, a tangerine sun
spilled light over the balustrade.

Ah! —There were times like that
on icy cold days.

冬の長門峡

長門峡に、水は流れてありにけり。
寒い寒い日なりき。

われは料亭にありぬ。
酒酌みてありぬ。

われのほか別に、
客とてもなかりけり。

水は、恰も魂あるものの如く、
流れ流れてありにけり。

やがても密柑の如き夕陽、
欄干にこぼれたり。

あゝ！　――そのやうな時もありき、
寒い寒い　日なりき。

Yoneko

The twenty-eight-year-old virgin
suffered from tuberculosis and had skinny calves.
Like a poplar tree, she was
standing along a desolate sidewalk.

The virgin's name was Yoneko.
In summer, her face looked dirty,
but in winter and autumn it was beautiful.
—She spoke in a frail voice.

It seemed to me that the twenty-eight-year-old virgin
might cure her illness by getting married.
And so, I often saw her
with this thought in mind . . .

However, not once did I say it aloud.
Not because it was difficult to bring it up
or that I feared doing so would just disappoint her,
but for some reason I never said anything.

The twenty-eight-year-old virgin
stood along the sidewalk
on a rainy afternoon like a poplar tree.
—I'd like to hear that frail voice once again . . .

米子

二十八歳のその処女は、
肺病やみで、腓は細かつた。
ポプラのやうに、人も通らぬ
歩道に沿つて、立つてゐた。

処女の名前は、米子と云つた。
夏には、顔が、汚れてみえたが、
冬だの秋には、きれいであつた。
——かぼそい声をしてをつた。

二十八歳のその処女は、
お嫁に行けば、その病気は
癒るかに思はれた。と、さう思ひながら
私はたびたび処女をみた……

しかし一度も、さうと口には出さなかつた。
別に、云ひ出しにくいからといふのでもない
云つて却つて、落胆させてはと思つたからでもない、
なぜかしら、云はずじまひであつたのだ。

二十八歳のその処女は、
歩道に沿つて立つてゐた、
雨あがりの午後、ポプラのやうに。
——かぼそい声をもう一度、聞いてみたいと思ふのだ……

Noon

scene at The Circle Building

ah the twelve o'clock siren, the siren, the siren
they're coming out in droves, coming out, coming out
office workers on lunch break swinging, swinging
  their hands
one after another they keep coming out, coming out,
  coming out
a big building's tiny doorway, tiny and pitch black
the sky spreads with clouds, thin clouds, and dust is
  stirring up
whether by chance I look up or lower my gaze . . .
what am I, a cherry blossom, cherry blossom,
  cherry blossom
ah the twelve o'clock siren, the siren, the siren
they're coming out in droves, coming out, coming out
a big building's tiny doorway, tiny and pitch black
on the wind blowing in the sky, the siren echoes, echoes
  and fades

正午

丸ビル風景

あゝ十二時のサイレンだ、サイレンだサイレンだ
ぞろぞろぞろぞろ出てくるわ、出てくるわ出て
　くるわ
月給取の午休み、ぷらりぷらりと手を振つて
あとからあとから出てくるわ、出てくるわ出て
　くるわ
大きなビルの真ッ黒い、小ッちやな小ッちやな
　出入口
空はひろびろ薄曇り、薄曇り、埃りも少々立つて
　ゐる
ひよんな目付で見上げても、眼を落としても……
なんのおのれが桜かな、桜かな桜かな
あゝ十二時のサイレンだ、サイレンだサイレンだ
ぞろぞろぞろぞろ出てくるわ、出てくるわ出て
　くるわ
大きなビルの真ッ黒い、小ッちやな小ッちやな
　出入口
空吹く風にサイレンは、響き響きて消えてゆく
　かな

Kasuga Rhapsody

1

When someone you love dies,
you have to commit suicide.

When someone you love dies,
there is no other way.

But even so, if your karma(?) is deep
and you're trying to carry on,

you will have a sense of service.
You will have a sense of service.

Because the one you love has died,
because they have surely died,

since you can't do anything about it,
for their sake, for their sake,

you must develop a sense of service.
You must develop a sense of service.

春日狂想

1

愛するものが死んだ時には、
自殺しなけあなりません。

愛するものが死んだ時には、
それより他に、方法がない。

けれどもそれでも、業（？）が深くて、
なほもながらふことともなつたら、

奉仕の気持に、なることなんです。
奉仕の気持に、なることなんです。

愛するものは、死んだのですから、
たしかにそれは、死んだのですから、

もはやどうにも、ならぬのですから、
そのもののために、そのもののために、

奉仕の気持に、ならなけあならない。
奉仕の気持に、ならなけあならない。

2

I felt that I wanted to serve,
but I can't do anything special.

So now I read books more carefully.
So now I'm more polite to people.

Taking a proper walk,
weaving straw with reverence—

it's like I'm a toy soldier,
and every day is a Sunday.

I walk leisurely in the shrine sunlight,
greet acquaintances,

become friends with the old candy seller,
scatter beans for the pigeons,

and when it gets too bright, crawl into the shade
to look again at the earth and greenery.

The moss feels really cool,
and today is beautiful beyond words.

Visitors walk by in droves.
I don't pay them any mind.

2

奉仕の気持になりはなつたが、
さて格別の、ことも出来ない。

そこで以前より、本なら熟読。
そこで以前より、人には丁寧。

テムポ正しき散歩をなして
麦稈真田を敬虔に編み——

まるでこれでは、玩具の兵隊、
まるでこれでは、毎日、日曜。

神社の日向を、ゆるゆる歩み、
知人に遇へば、につこり致し、

飴売爺々と、仲よしになり、
鳩に豆なぞ、パラパラ撒いて、

まぶしくなつたら、日蔭に這入り、
そこで地面や草木を見直す。

苔はまことに、ひんやりいたし、
いはうやうなき、今日の麗日。

参詣人等もぞろぞろ歩き、
わたしは、なんにも腹が立たない。

((Life is truly a fleeting dream,
like the beauty of a rubber balloon.))

Rising into the sky, shining, disappearing—
Hey, how are you doing today?

It's been a while. How are things?
Let's go have tea someplace nearby.

I bravely enter the teahouse,
but there's nothing to talk about.

I smoke a cigarette
and muster an indescribable resolve—

It's really lively outside!
—Well, give my best to your wife.

Please write when you go abroad.
And don't drink too much.

Horse-drawn carriages pass by. Trains, too.
Life is just like a wedding reception.

Dazzling, beautiful, she bows her head,
but would you get bored if you let her talk?

Still, she puts your heart in a daze.
Life is just like a wedding reception.

((まことに人生、一瞬の夢、
ゴム風船の、美しさかな。))

空に昇つて、光つて、消えて——
やあ、今日は、御機嫌いかが。

久しぶりだね、その後どうです。
そこらの何処かで、お茶でも飲みましよ。

勇んで茶店に這入りはすれど、
ところで話は、とかくないもの。

煙草なんぞを、くさくさ吹かし、
名状しがたい覚悟をなして、——

戸外はまことに賑やかなこと！
——ではまたそのうち、奥さんによろしく、

外国に行つたら、たよりを下さい。
あんまりお酒は、飲まんがいいよ。

馬車も通れば、電車も通る。
まことに人生、花嫁御寮。

まぶしく、美しく、はた俯いて、
話をさせたら、でもうんざりか？

それでも心をポーッとさせる、
まことに、人生、花嫁御寮。

3

So, everyone,
without being overly happy or sad,
at the right tempo, let's shake hands.

In other words, understand
that what we lack is honesty.

Okay, everyone, okay. All together now—
at the right tempo, let's shake hands.

3

ではみなさん、
喜び過ぎず悲しみ過ぎず、
テムポ正しく、握手をしませう。

つまり、我等に欠けてるものは、
実直なんぞと、心得まして。

ハイ、ではみなさん、ハイ、御一緒に——
テムポ正しく、握手をしませう。

Frog Voice

The heavens cover the earth,
and on the earth there happens to be a pond.
On that pond tonight a night frog croaks . . .
—What is it crying for?

That voice, does it come from the sky
and leave for the sky?
The heavens cover the earth,
and a frog croaks on the water surface.

Even if it's too humid in this region,
to our weary hearts
the pillars still seem too dry,

our heads feel heavy, shoulders stiff.
But when night comes, the frog croaks,
and that voice rushes across the water toward dark clouds.

蛙声

天は地を蓋ひ、
そして、地には偶々池がある。
その池で今夜一と夜さ蛙は鳴く……
——あれは、何を鳴いてるのであらう？

その声は、空より来り、
空へと去るのであらう？
天は地を蓋ひ、
そして蛙声は水面に走る。

よし此の地方が湿潤に過ぎるとしても、
疲れたる我等が心のためには、
柱は猶、余りに乾いたものと感はれ、

頭は重く、肩は凝るのだ。
さて、それなのに夜が来れば蛙は鳴き、
その声は水面に走つて暗雲に迫る。

Postscript

The majority of the poems collected here were published after *Goat Songs*. The oldest was written in 1925, and the most recent was written in 1937. I say this in the introduction, but *Goat Songs* includes poems written from the spring of 1924 to the spring of 1930.

If writing poetry can be called a poetic life, then my poetic life has already lasted twenty-three years. If we should call it a poetic life from the day I decided to make poetry my main occupation, then I have lived a poetic life for fifteen years.

During those long and short years, I have felt and thought many things. Just thinking about giving an overview of it now makes me shudder. That's why I have no intention of talking about it. I just want to say that from the day I was sure that my personality was best suited to poetry, I made poetry my profession.

Now, I have put together the manuscript for this collection of poems, entrusted it to my friend Hideo Kobayashi, and am leaving my life in Tokyo after thirteen years to retreat to my hometown. I don't have any new plans but have decided to finally immerse myself in a life of poetry.

So, what will happen after this . . . the thought leaves me dumbfounded.

Farewell, Tokyo! Oh, my youth!

[September 23, 1937]

後記

茲に收めたのは、「山羊の歌」以後に發表したものの過半數である。作つたのは、最も古いのでは大正十四年のもの、最も新しいのでは昭和十二年のものがある。序でだから云ふが、「山羊の歌」には大正十三年春の作から昭和五年春迄のものを收めた。

詩を作りさへすればそれで詩生活といふことが出來れば、私の詩生活も既に二十三年を經た。もし詩を以て本職とする覺悟をした日からを詩生活と稱すべきなら、十五年間の詩生活である。

長いといへば長い、短いといへば短いその年月の間に、私の感じたこと考へたことは少くない。今その概略を述べてみようかと、一寸思つてみるだけでもゾッとする程だ。私は何にも、だから語らうとは思はない。たゞ私は、私の個性が詩に最も適することを、確實に確かめた日から詩を本職としたのであつたことだけを、ともかくも云つてをきたい。

私は今、此の詩集の原稿を纏め、友人小林秀雄に託し、東京十三年間の生活に別れて、鄉里に引籠るのである。別に新しい計畫があるのでもないが、いよいよ詩生活に沈潜しようと思つてゐる。

扨、此の後どうなることか……それを思へば茫洋とする。

さらば東京！　おゝわが青春！

〔一九三七、九、二三〕

Notes on the Poems

Source materials for these notes include those mentioned in the Introduction—primarily Shōhei Ōoka's biography and *Shinpen Nakahara Chūya Zenshū* (Collected Works of Chūya Nakahara, New Edition), but also books and essays by Tetsutarō Kawakami, Saburō Kawamoto, Tōru Kitagawa, Hideo Kobayashi, Haruo Satō, Juntarō Tanaka, Kunio Yanagita, and Hirō Yoshida. The first date indicates when the poem was drafted, the second when first published.

GOAT SONGS

Dusk on a Spring Day

c.1924 / June 1933

Together with "The Moon," "Circus" and "Spring Night," one of four Dadaist poems that open the collection. With his katakana version of the English term "thrown underhand" Chūya seems to be mocking Western imports to Japanese parlance. Critic Haruo Satō said the blue sky in Mallarmé's "L'Azur" ("The Azure") is a likely source for this poem's surreal haze.

The Moon

c.1927–1929 / September 1929

In his diary of 1927, Chūya made the notation "Salomé . . . Oscar Wilde." Shōhei Ōoka noticed the textual correspondences between this poem and the play, which had been performed in translation on a number of Japanese stages in the 1910s and 20s: the moon is a symbolic plot device, while the "doubting foster father" surely refers to Herod Antipas, and the "seven celestial nymphs" to the Dance of the Seven Veils. Published with six other poems in the September 1929 issue of *Shi to shiron* (Poetry and Poetics).

Circus

c.1925 / October 1929

This poem's musical *kōgo* combines with regular 7/5 morae to produce a quality that resembles the speaking style of kabuki actors and reveals Chūya's respect for Verlaine's powers of music in poetry. Critic Hirō Yoshida noted that, while some may feel "brown war" refers to the Russo-Japanese War of 1904–1905 in which the Japanese soldiers wore khaki, Chūya first published the poem in the journal *Shi to shiron* as "Untitled," and its description of a circus may in fact be symbolic, not historical, expressing the movements of the speaker's consciousness. The clowns here absent appear in later works.

Spring Night

1926 / October 1929

One of the poems from this period in which Chūya attempts to combine a variety of styles, including French Symbolism, classical Japanese and Chinese. It employs the Dadaist/Surrealist device of synesthesia, as embodied in Rimbaud's sonnet "Voyelles" ("Vowels"), which the poet read in 1925. Critics suggest a Chinese, Arabian or French court setting, with the latter reinforced by Chūya's diary entries of 1926 that reveal a longing for Paris.

Morning Song

May 1926 / c. 1928

Inspired by the Petrarchan sonnets of Baudelaire and Rimbaud. Chūya showed this piece, composed in 1926, to Hideo Kobayashi—the first poem he showed anyone after his arrival in Tokyo. "With 'Morning Song,'" he later wrote to a friend, "I had more or less found my way, but when I thought of how much trouble it had taken me to write a mere fourteen lines, I felt exhausted." The poem is universally recognized as one of Chūya's finest. Representing a conscious break from the influence of Dada and the French Symbolists, it offers a paradigm of his ability to combine classical language and strict 5/7 morae lineation with a "new style" sensibility of highly subjective topicality and point of view. Set to music by Saburō Moroi—a key collaborative milestone for Chūya—and performed in May of 1928.

Deathbed

1926 / c.1928

Written in *bungo* (literary Japanese), this poem follows the *ki-shō-ten-ketsu* (introduction-development-turn-conclusion) structure of the *zakku*, a Classical Chinese quatrain form that, per Ōoka, jars against its modern subject—a prostitute of Yokohama's red-light district, which Chūya frequented. In a letter to Masaoka Chūzaburō dated January 15, 1927, he wrote, "I think I'm going to Yokohama or somewhere today . . . Yokohama is the place of water sounds, of joys and sorrows, a little fantasy of my mother's childhood and the purity of history, as it were." His affinity for the city likely stemmed from his mother Fuku, born (1879) and raised in her early years there. Set to music by Saburō Moroi and performed with "Morning Song" on May 21, 1928.

Urban Summer Night

c.1926 / September 1929

A shift away from Dada toward urban realism. If the draft year is correct, Chūya was already living in Tokyo. The scene he paints of city dwellers stumbling home late reflects the Taishō-era nightlife boom (which for Chūya often meant Ginza bars), but has felt uncannily contemporary to every generation of readers since the poem's publication in *Shi to shiron*. The formal collars may suggest the men are returning from a colleague's wedding.

One Autumn Day

1926 / July 1929

A companion piece to "Deathbed" and understood to be about the cosmopolitan Yokohama port area. Includes the English words "Sirens," "platform" and "Yankees" in katakana. The final stanza makes this poem one of Chūya's most popular and iconic: according to critic Hirō Yoshida, its rhythm echoes Verlaine's *Romances sans Paroles*. First published in the second issue of *Hakuchigun* (Band of Idiots).

Twilight

November 1925 / September 1929

Ōoka tells us that soon after Yasuko left him, the poet moved to a boarding house in Momozono, a residential area built on reclaimed rice fields near Nakano Station on Tokyo's Chuo Line. Behind it was a lotus pond. The poem seems to affirm a determination, despite his restless spirit, not to retreat to rural Yamaguchi.

Midnight Thoughts

c.1928–1929 / July 1929

"Margaret" is Gretchen, the lover of the protagonist in Goethe's *Faust*. The poem may be read with that epic play's imagery in mind, as Chūya reveals his post-Yasuko romantic despair through Faust's doomed love. Chūya surely developed an interest in Goethe through Baudelaire, who read him obsessively. Published in *Hakuchigun*.

Winter Night Rain

c.1926–1927 / November 1929

The 10th line of Rimbaud's "Brussels" has flocks of birds crying in nonsense vocalizations: "o iaio, iaio! . . . " Chūya translated the poem sometime between 1929 and 1933. Rain, here representing existential weight, is a Rimbaudian motif that Chūya internalized.

Homecoming

c.1927–1928 / May 1930

A rare Shakespearean-like sonnet by Chūya, this poem reveals his homesickness for Yamaguchi. Set to music by Seiichirō Utsumi and performed by the musical group Surya at their fifth concert on May 20, 1930.

Tremendous Twilight

? / July 1929

Chūya wrote this poem on a piece of paper when he met Yasuo Murai, who would later become a member of the Band of Idiots group. Apparently, it only survived because Murai held onto it. First published in *Hakuchigun*, then again in *Kigen* (Era) in 1933, and a third time in *Aoi Hana* (Blue Flower) in 1934.

Song of Summer Going By

c.1921–1922 / September 1929

Biographer Juntarō Tanaka says the poet here reminisces on Chūya's Yamaguchi childhood. The last line is often cited by his enthusiasts as one that is characteristically Chūya.

Dreary Morning

c.1926–1927 / September 1929

Suggests a hybrid sonnet—perhaps Petrarchan with three lines omitted. Of special note is the eleventh line, composed entirely of a long ellipsis, which possibly mirrors Chūya's post-Yasuko emotional silences.

Song for a Summer Day

c.1932 / April 1933

The summer motif reflects renewed energy after a 1931 slump in productivity. Published in the inaugural issue of *Kigen*, which became a key outlet for early modernists. Written around the time Chūya finished editing *Goat Songs*, whose publication he delayed until June 1934, as more individual poems were finding their way into print.

Evening Sun

c. April–May 1929 / July 1929

Echoes Verlaine's twilight themes. Ōoka, who became famous for his anti-war novel *Nobi* (*Fires on the Plain*, 1951) and many successive works, said that he got through difficult times on the battlefield by humming a line from this poem.

Port Town Autumn

c.1926 / c.1929

This ironically humorous poem is thought to express Chūya's sense of alienation, with the oft-cited chair perhaps representative of himself, of living as an outsider. The pipes are *kiseru*, a long-stemmed tobacco pipe with a small metal bowl that carries a classical atmosphere at pleasant odds with the free verse *kōgo* in which the piece is written. A nod to Edo nostalgia amid Taishō modernity.

Sigh

c.1927 / July 1929

Published in *Hakuchigun*. This sprawling surrealistic fourteen-liner expresses an imagined nostalgia for the Russian plains, with Chekhovian scenery superimposed on the Japanese countryside. It is dedicated to Chūya's friend Tetsutarō Kawakami, a fellow member of the Band of Idiots coterie, whose friendship and support were vital to the realization of *Goat Songs*. Kawakami wrote the first essay in his collection *Nihon no autosaidā* (Japan's Outsiders, 1959) about Chūya.

Spring Memory

1926 / October 1929

Written in *bungo* of mostly 5/7 morae with substitutions. The word "quadrille" would have been new to most readers and gives the poem an exotic atmosphere of French antiquity. Although the setting seems rural, pastoral pockets—including fields of blooming lotus flowers—could be found all over Shōwa-period Tokyo.

Autumn Night Sky

c.1928 / July 1929

A subtle paean to Chūya's cosmic loneliness, published in *Hakuchigun*. Shadow festivals are more simple affairs held in alternating years with main festivals and, according to folklorist Kunio Yanagita, date back to the Muromachi era (1336–1573).

Hangover

c. April–June 1932? / June 1934 (Goat Songs)

Despite—or perhaps partly because of—its brevity, this remains one of Chūya's most well-known poems. He himself felt it worthy enough to use as the end point of Early Poems. Ōoka claims the brevity of this "drunken epiphany" mirrors Chūya's exhaustion, although it surely also stands as a literal representation of his 1932 binge-drinking phase.

Boyhood

c.1927–1928 / June 1934 (Goat Songs)

Surely inspired by Rimbaud's prose poem "Enfance" ("Childhood"). Chūya considered this as a possible title for the *Goat Songs* collection.

Blind Autumn

c.1929–1930 / April 1930

Published together with nine other poems in the last issue of *Hakuchigun* (No.6), after which the Band of Idiots coterie dissolved. An elegy to youth and Chūya's failed relationship with Yasuko. The "faith" or self-confidence promoted in the second section derives from Chūya's reading of Verlaine's "Sagesse" ("Wisdom"), the exclamations in the third from his complicated relationship with Catholicism. Although not devout, he regarded it as the perfect religion.

My Smoking

c.1929–1930 / April 1930

Published in *Hakuchigun*. Although the poem is composed of 14 lines, Chūya divides it into 7-line stanzas, making it something of an anti-sonnet wherein the "you" is, as ever, the object of his lost love, Yasuko.

Darling

1929 or 1930 / April 1930

Published in *Hakuchigun*. Set to music by Saburō Moroi and performed on June 5th, 1935, followed by a radio broadcast reading in November. 妹 (*Imōto*) in the poem's Japanese title means literally "younger sister," but was also used in poetry and antiquity to signify a lover or wife.

Self-Portrait on a Cold Night

January 1929 / April 1929

Published in the inaugural issue of *Hakuchigun*. The first part of a triptych of which the second and third parts were not included in *Goat Songs*. Poet and critic Tōru Kitagawa called the last two lines of this poem, which is composed mostly of *bungo* and regular 5/7 morae, "a prayer-like longing that can be nothing but prayer itself."

Tree Shade

July 1929 / September 1929

Between the second and third drafts, Chūya deleted all punctuation—a trick he learned from Rimbaud—in order to liberate rhythm. Published in the third issue of *Hakuchigun*.

Lost Hope

c.1929–1930 / April 1930

One of the ten poems Chūya published in the last issue of *Hakuchigun*. The theme seems tied to the magazine's untimely end. Seiichirō

Utsumi gave it a brief afterlife by scoring it in May.

Summer

August 1929 / September 1929

A Petrarchan sonnet. Ōoka claims that the poem's relentlessly dark mood represents a final exorcism of Yasuko. On August 13, 1937, not long before Chūya's death, poet Kusano Shinpei recited this poem on a radio program, and it made a deep impression on the writer Shimaki Kensaku, contributing to Chūya's late fame.

Image

c. 1929–1930 / June 1934 (Goat Songs)

Chūya is a master at rendering landscapes that Japanese readers find familiar or nostalgic. Here he blends those of Yamaguchi and Tokyo.

Michiko

c. November 1929 / January 1930

According to Ōoka, the title refers to Michiko Hayama, the screen name of Seiko Ishikawa, another film actress who lived in Kyoto at the same lodgings as Yasuko. Chūya later described her to Ōoka as an ideal woman. She lived for some years in a *ménage à trois* relationship with her older sister Chiyoko and Chiyoko's husband, the novelist Junichiro Tanizaki, who apparently preferred Seiko as a sexual partner in his masochistic games. Tanizaki wrote some of her film roles, and she was the model for the teenage bar hostess protagonist in his 1924 novel *Chijin no ai* (*Naomi*). Chūya here intentionally uses dated or overly formal diction and syntax.

To Ruined Sorrow . . .

1929 or 1930 / April 1930

Published in *Hakuchigun*. Composed entirely of 7/5 morae lines with 8/5 substitutions. Chūya achieves an ironic effect here, as elsewhere, by combining *kōgo* with traditional structure. His most famous poem.

Untitled

c.1929 / June 1929

An early free verse experiment. Part III began as a standalone with the title "To My Poetry Friends" that Chūya published independently in the first issue of *Hakuchigun.*

The Advance of Night

c.1929 / April 1930

Night as Chūya's existential cloak. Featured in the final issue of *Hakuchigun,* set to music by Seiichirō Utsumi, and performed by Surya on May 20th, 1930. The group's modernist bent helped to amplify the poet's reach.

Sinner's Song

c.1929–1930 / April 1930

Dedicated to poet-scholar Rokurō Abe, younger brother of the philosopher Jirō Abe, who was famous for his *Santarō no nikki* (*Santarō's Diary, 1914).* Described by Ōoka as Chūya's kindred spirit in sin, Rokurō was also a member of the Band of Idiots. The opening lines seem to derive from Baudelaire's "L'Ennemi" ("The Enemy"), which Chūya translated, having doubtless already read Kafū Nagai's version of it years earlier in *Sangoshū* (Collection of Coral, 1913).

Autumn

c.1929 / November 1929

An early example of Chūya writing with mature ease in free verse *kōgo.* The traditional clothing evokes a Taishō period casualness.

Elegy for the Town of Shura

c.1928–1929 / c.November 1929

Ōoka tells us that, according to Fumio Takamori, Chūya's original title for *Goat Songs* was *Shura Street Songs.* The "Shura" of this poem is supposedly the same as that from Kenji Miyazawa's "Spring and

Shura," wherein the name is associated with Ashura, one of the eight great deities of Buddhism, whose path is one of conflict. Indeed, the setting seems a projection of the poet's inner chaos. In the spring of 1928, Chūya began living at the creative hub lodgings of Takakatsu Sekiguchi—to whom he dedicated the poem and who later became a senior government official—in what is now the Suginami Ward of Tokyo.

Snowy Evening
c. January–February 1930 / April 1930
Chūya was influenced by the folk lyricism of Hakushu Kitahara and here improvises on lines from a piece in his second collection, *Omoide* (Memories, 1911), which Chūya may have read in 1929. Published in the last issue of *Hakuchigun* (No. 6).

Song of Upbringing
c. January–February 1930 / April 1930
A diary entry of 1927 in which Chūya mentions that he read *Senshin kabanashi* (Cleansing Songs) in 1927 suggests he had known Hakushu Kitahara's work for many years. The title may derive from Hakushu's *Waga sei hitachi* (My Hitachi Life). Published in the last issue of *Hakuchigun* (No. 6).

Now is the Hour . . .
c. January–February 1930 / April 1930
Chūya gathered elements from the first two stanzas of Baudelaire's "Harmonie du Soir" to compose the first stanza of this sonnet.

Sheep Song
c.1931–1932 / June 1934 (Goat Songs)
Chūya underwent a spiritual turn around the time this poem was written. The sheep here is generally understood by critics to be a Judeo-Christian symbol of his sacrificial self, with poet-scholar

Etsurō Sakamoto further suggesting that the communion with the nine-year-old girl represents a moment of spiritual grace. The epigraph to section three is from Baudelaire's "L'Ennemi" ("The Enemy"), for which I used Richard Howard's translation.

Atrophy
c.1932 / c. April 1934
Written after a year of relative poetic stagnation during which Chūya had become immersed in his language school studies. He originally wrote the Catherine de Medici epigraph in French but changed it to Japanese for subsequent drafts.

Voice of Life
c. April–June 1932 / June 1934 (Goat Songs)
One of only three poems in *Goat Songs* for which no draft or published version has ever been found, the others being "Hangover" and "Sheep Song." The first draft was likely completed just before Chūya began editing the collection. This poem's philosophical contents are understood to derive from Blaise Pascal. In December of 1927, Chūya read a digest of Pascal by Miki Kiyoshi, who introduced the philosopher's work to Japan after having studied him in Paris from 1922 to 1925.

SONGS OF BYGONE DAYS

Shame
c. November 1935 / c. January 1936
As a memorial to his son Fumiya, who had died in November 1936, Chūya replaced "Emptiness" with this as the opening poem and added the subtitle when he arranged the manuscript in the summer of 1937. The dead children are not a reference to Fumiya, since the poem was written before his death. "Astrakhan" refers to the wool of the famous sheep of that region whose lambs are slaughtered soon after birth; as analogs to the children, they contrast with the ele-

phants, who embody strength and longevity. Some critics recognize an influence from Rimbaud's prose poem "Enfance" ("Childhood").

Emptiness

February 1926 / March 1935

One of the oldest poems in the collection and originally intended to be the first, which indicates its thematic importance to Chūya. This sonnet combines elements of Dadaism with difficult *kango* (Chinese words), the latter an influence of contemporaries like Kenji Miyazawa. Chūya set many poems in Yokohama, a city where he had family connections (his mother was born and his grandfather buried there), and he spent much of his leisure time soaking up its decadent and exotic atmosphere, especially in the red-light district with his favorite prostitute. The "rhomboids" of the closing couplet may refer to a diamond pattern he saw on a woman's kimono.

Late Night Rain

c.1929 / August, 1936

By the time he wrote this poem, Chūya was already reading Verlaine and surely knew his "Il pleure dans mon cœur" ("It's Raining in My Heart") from the collection *Romances Sans Paroles* (*Songs Without Words*, 1874). The French original includes an epigraph by Rimbaud—"Il pleut doucement sur la ville" ("It's raining gently on the city")—which suggests he inspired it. Numerous composers set Verlaine's poem to music, most notably Fauré and Debussy.

Early Spring Wind

1928 / 1935

Published in the May 13 issue of *Teikoku daigaku shinbun* (Imperial University Newspaper), predecessor to *Tōdai shinbun* (Tokyo University Newspaper). The student in charge asked Chūya to change the title, saying that it was no longer early spring. Chūya's response: "It is outrageous that [you] think of poetry as if it were a yukata sales pitch or something. This shows a low level of culture." The scenery is inspired by that around Hiroshima, which Chūya saw through a train window on his way back to Yamaguchi from Tokyo, and wrote down on a postcard addressed to his poet friend Yoshihiro Yasuhara after visiting him in Kyoto. Yasuhara had helped Chūya get *Goat Songs* published the previous year.

Moon
c.1924–1925 / c.1934
Written around the same time as the "Moon" of *Goat Songs*, this similarly abstruse Dada-influenced poem reveals elements of Chūya's early life as the son of a country physician. Chūya's younger brother Shirō wrote years later: "At that time, hospitals had a *saiseiba*. It was a room where bandages, gauze, cotton wool, etc. were washed and disinfected. Water was poured into a disinfection pot with a diameter of one meter, brought to a boil, and dirty items were boiled. The stench was from carbolic acid, and the room, filled with steam, had a lime-like smell." The medal appears to have something in common with the button in "Moonlit Beach."

Blue Eyes
c. September 1935 / 1935
The title does not refer to a foreigner. If, instead, "blue" means "young" (an old Japanese analogy) as it does in "Early Spring Wind," it may refer to the poet himself, his sense of a fading youthful vigor. By this time, Chūya had joined the coterie of the magazine *Shiki* (Four Seasons), and this poem's general accessibility may suggest he was starting to write with the "general reader" in mind.

Memory From the Age of Three
c.1935–1936 / June 1936
Recounts a formative experience from the poet's infancy, like a moment out of Rimbaud's acclaimed prose poem "Enfance"

("Childhood"), which Chūya had revisited in the 1930s. Here he successfully reinhabits his youthful hypersensitivity, one derived in part from living in isolation much of the time. Even after he entered elementary school, his father rarely let him play outside.

June Rain
c. April 1936 / July 1936
This meticulously rendered sonnet first appeared in the July issue of *Bungakukai* (Literary Society) magazine as an entry for the Sixth Bungakukai Prize, coming in second to Kanoko Okamoto's long prose piece "Tsuru wa yamiki" ("The Dying Crane"), a memorial to the tragic literary genius Ryūnosuke Akutagawa. The child is either Fumiya, the poet, or a blend of the two, while the woman is likely Yasuko.

Rainy Day
c. 1936 / June 1936
Notable for Chūya's use of the asterisk to create a more pronounced conceptual division between stanzas—possibly a nod to Apollinaire's visual poetry. The Japanese phrase 舌あまりの幼 (*shita amari no yō*), literally "a child with too much tongue," refers to one who has not yet learned to speak fluently. Anecdotal evidence confirms that Chūya struggled to express himself at an early age.

Spring
c. 1925–1926 / September 1929
First appeared in *Shi to shiron*. Ōoka suggests this poem captures Chūya's post-Dada pivot, blending pastoral calm with urban undertones.

Song for a Spring Day
c. March 1929 / May 1929
A moment of springtime optimism in the midst of personal chaos.

Like so many of Chūya's poems, this Petrarchan sonnet combines *kōgo* and *bungo*, echoing his early translations of Baudelaire. It first appeared in *Bungakukai*.

Summer Night

1925 / September 1929

Bears a coincidental resemblance to the villanelle—a difficult form of French origin that weaves refrains through five tercets and a quatrain—but Chūya had not encountered one when he wrote it. Rather, as Ōoka tells us, the poem's repetitions stem from a musicality honed in Yamaguchi via folk songs and tanka thematics.

Song of the Young Beast

c. June 1936 / August 1936

More than any poem in Chūya's oeuvre, this one perhaps best represents the poet's paradoxical artistic philosophy. To paraphrase from the Introduction, here is the world before the word, while the beast is, of course, Chūya himself, his primal creativity unleashed in the wake of Fumiya's birth. Before World War II, fire pots were to be found beside Japanese hearths and cooking areas. Made of clay or tile and lidded, they were used to extinguish embers.

The Child

c.1934–1935 / June 1935

Chūya's subconscious projection of fatherhood, the child prefigures Fumiya. Again, one feels the influence of Rimbaud's "L'Enfance," which the poet revisited in translation around this time. Published in *Bungakukai*.

Winter Day Memory

December 1935 / c.1936

In January of 1915, Chūya's younger brother Tsugurō died. It was the catalyst for his first attempt at poetry—an elegy—and also a harbinger to the early demise of countless family (seven in his brief lifetime), friends and colleagues, most painfully his son Fumiya. The poem includes various facts surrounding the tragedy, including his father being away at the time.

Autumn Day

c.1936 / October 1936

A Petrarchan sonnet that imitates the "separated writing" technique of Hyogo writer and critic Hōmei Iwano (1873–1920). Chūya creates a unique rhythm and temporal obscurity by blurring syntax with inserted spaces, lack of punctuation, and varying the number of characters on each line.

Icy Night

c. January 1936 / February 1936

During what was, per his diary entries, an emotionally difficult year, Chuya became a member of the polished *Shiki* coterie in 1935. This was his first publication in their magazine.

Winter Dawn

November 1935 / April 1936

Published in the poetry journal *Rekitei* (Trajectory) (1935–present), of whose coterie Chūya was a founding member. Chūya employs a characteristic rhetorical device in the second stanza, using the verb "fled" to mean not physical departure but an absence from perception—a nod to his fascination with Buddhist impermanence. Like the rest of the landscape, the forest and farmer have not yet awakened.

As an Old Man

October 1928 / May 1930

At the end of 1927, Chūya began meeting regularly with the musical group Surya, led by composer Saburō Moroi (1903–1977), whose fondness for dissonance and tonal drift appealed to the poet's own avant-garde tastes. Moroi set this poem to music, and the group performed it at its fifth recital on May 20, 1930, together with "Lost Hope" from *Goat Songs*.

On the Lake

June 1930 / August 1930

Published in the magazine *Kirinohana* (Paulownia Flowers), whose Kyoto-based coterie offered Chūya a new stage following the collapse of *Hakuchigun*. Written in the voice of a woman and perhaps born of Chūya's anguish over Yasuko having that year rejected him for the last time. This book version of the poem is distinctly different from the magazine original and was probably found amongst unpublished drafts by his editors.

Winter Night

January 1933 / April 1935

Maybe as a subtle and ironic gesture of rebellion, apolitical Chūya published this poem in nationalist *Nihon shi* (Japanese Poetry) magazine. One of countless pieces written during his 1933 post-language-school recovery from poetic stagnation.

Autumn News

c. Autumn 1933 / July 1934

In a letter to Kobayashi after arriving in Tokyo, Chūya revealed his newcomer status when he mistakenly referred to advertising balloons as "air signs."

Bone

April 28, 1934 / June 1934

A stark self-portrait penned after a boozy night on the town and published in the journal *Kigen* (Era), whose modernist crowd embraced its raw vitality. This poem is rare in that Chūya wrote the exact date he composed it on the original manuscript.

Autumn Day Madness

c. September 1935 / November 1935

The reference to war in Europe is an example of "cosmopolitan" Chūya. Complicating his generally bohemian persona are such occasional foreign references and words that want to suggest an urban sophistication, that the poet keeps abreast of world news—in this case, Germany's declared intent to rearm itself. Chūya clearly admired the beatnik philosophy of Diogenes (404–323 BC) and the Cynics school, who eschewed the burdens of culture and conventional morality.

Korean Woman

c. April 1935 / May 1935

Since Yamaguchi is close to Korea, their populations have co-mingled since antiquity. It is well known, for example, that the Ōuchi clan was proud of having Silla ancestors. Here, as elsewhere, the poet's playful use of Western punctuation marks hints at concrete poetry such as Apollinaire's *Calligrammes*, where typeface and word arrangement contribute to meaning. In the original manuscript, the dots that underscore the poem are bigger and more widely spaced than the ellipses. Reminiscent of "Dreary Morning" in this regard.

A Dream I Awoke to On a Summer Night

c. August 1935 / October 1935

In his correspondence with Yoshihiro Yasuhara, Chūya refers to radio broadcasts of the summer National Junior High School (now High School) Baseball Championship, known as the Koshien, and writes in his diary that he went to prefectural qualifying games near his home in Yamaguchi. Published in *Shiki* magazine, whose coterie Chūya had joined. That year, he made multiple diary entries on insomnia.

Spring and Baby

c.1935 / April 1935

Published in *Bungakukai* and two months later as a song. The latter Chūya clearly premeditated with his choices of rhythm and repetition, and the general musicality echoes his Surya days with Moroi. Ōoka links this piece to Chūya's joy at impending fatherhood.

Skylarks

c.1935 / April 1935

Published in *Bungakukai* as a companion piece to "Spring and Baby." Hideo Kobayashi had become editor-in-chief of the magazine that January, giving Chūya an open publication venue of which he took great advantage. Old friend, new gatekeeper.

Early Summer Night

June 6, 1935 / August 1935

Published in *Bungakukai*. The twenty-ninth poem, and therefore at the exact center of the collection. This might be indicative of a deliberate midpoint pivot, reflecting Chūya's balance of joy at Fumiya's impending birth and fear due to his health dips that year. The exact date suggests a rare moment of sharp focus amidst his typical booze-fueled and fragmentary nature.

Northern Sea

February 1935 / May 1935

With the sea as Chūya's vast existential obverse to the cloistered despair of "Hangover," its mirror piece from *Goat Songs*, this poem also became one of his most popular. Published in the first issue of *Rekitei*, which spotlighted it.

Song of Innocence

December 1935 / January 1936

Published in *Bungei-hanron* (General Theories of Literature), co-founded by Toichirō Iwasa and Masayuki Jō. The line "When I think about it, I've come a long way" has since been variously used as a title—in 1978 by folk group Kaien-tai, and then in 1980–1981 by Shochiku Studio for a movie and subsequent TV series starring Tetsuya Takeda.

Quiet

c. April 1935 / March 1936

Published in the first issue of the second volume of *Rekitei*. The Yamaguchi-born haiku poet Santōka Taneda (1882–1940) never met Chūya in person but is said to have commented regarding the lines about the dripping faucet, "This feels like a haiku."

Clown Song

c.1934 / June 1934

Chūya wrote no fewer than ten poems about clowns or in a clownish tone that year—a mask of mirth amid personal lows. The "thirteenth son" is a playful reference to Schubert having been his parents' twelfth child.

Memory

c.1936 / August 1936

Many critics believe that the brick factory and general scenery match those of the seaside at Ube, Yamaguchi, which Chūya may have visited with his father. The city produced unique—and cheap—pink bricks by mixing red coal ash and lime without firing it.

Late Summer Heat

c.1936 / September 1936

Published in *Fujin koron* (Woman's View, 1916-), marking Chūya's debut in a women's magazine. *Fujin koron* was one of the major intellectual, feminist women's magazines of the Taishō era and onward.

New Year's Eve Bell
c. December 1935 / January 1936
Published, appropriately, in the New Year issue of *Shiki*, whose coterie Chūya had joined the previous year.

Ode to Snow
c. March 1936 / May 1936
Published in *Shiki*. Tadao "Gengo" Ōtaka (1672–February 4, 1703) was one of the 47 rōnin who took part in the legendary Akō vendetta, which by all accounts happened in the snow. He was also a talented haiku poet. The Russian scenery was likely inspired from Chūya's readings about the Bolshevik Revolution.

My Half Life
c. May 1936 / July 1936
This moment of self-reckoning was published in *Shiki*. The title echoes Pascal's *Pensées* (*Thoughts*), which Chūya had studied via Miki Kiyoshi's 1926 digest of the collection.

Single
April 1936 / c.1936
Chūya was married at the time he wrote the poem, so being single and on a borderline are understood as metaphors for existential solitude. The characters よそゆき ("formal") are marked with totens in the original manuscript to offset them from surrounding hiragana: よ、そ、ゆ、き、.

Spring Evening Nostalgia
c. 1936 / July 1936
Published in *Bungakukai*. Despite the distracting totens—an homage to the playful works of Edo period Buddhist poet-priest Issa—Chūya rigorously wrought this poem with formal tanka-like 7/5 morae phrasing. The public address of "everyone" foreshadows his

final communal plea at the end of "Kasuga Rhapsody."

Cloudy Sky

c. 1936 / July 1936

The only poem Chūya ever published in *Kaizō* (Modifications, 1919–1955), a general-purpose magazine that featured prose fiction, poetry, plays, literary criticism and commentaries by leading writers and intellectuals, many of whom had socialist beliefs or sympathies. As early as 1927, The Ministry of Home Affairs Information Bureau began banning particular issues on political and religious grounds; by the 1940s, contributors were being arrested, and the editor-in-chief and his staff were ultimately forced out and replaced.

To the Dragonflies

c. August 1936 / c. 1936

Published in *Murasaki* (Purple, 1934–present), an educational magazine aimed at female teachers. Ōoka sees the dragonflies as a motif of fleeting beauty that recalls Chūya's Yamaguchi summers.

I Will Never Return

c. 1936 / November 1936

In this rare prose poem directly inspired by Rimbaud's *Illuminations,* Chūya crafts a fantastical return to the formative years he spent in Kyoto as a young Dadaist (1923–25). Published in *Shiki.*

A Fairy Tale

c. 1936 / November 1936

Published in *Bungei-hanron,* this sonnet is universally recognized as one of Chūya's finest later works. Ōoka describes it as "a pagan creation myth," Kobayashi as Chūya's "most beautiful legacy." The setting derives from a site sacred to the poet—the Yoshiki River that flows through his hometown of Yuda-onsen. The Nakahara family cemetery is nearby.

Illusion
before September 1937 / November 1937
Ōoka suggests this captures the poet's late blurring of reality prior to his breakdown in January of 1937. Its ethereality echoes Verlaine's "Sagesse," one of Chūya's comfort reads. His editors found it amongst his papers post-mortem and then likely polished it before publication—first in *Bungakukai* and then in *Songs of Bygone Days.*

The Slut's Husband Sang
c. 1936 / November 1936
Published in *Rekitei*. Some critics believe the woman represents Yasuko. Chūya may have found inspiration for this work's plain speech and grit in poems by Jules Laforgue and Tristan Corbière that he had translated.

Song Without Words
c. 1936 / December 1936
In classical usage, the kanji 蒼 (*sō*) of the third line signified vibrant colors such as "lush green" (vegetation) and "deep blue" (sky, sea). But by the Edo period, it had picked up a figurative sense of faded vitality—especially in poetry—and could be read as "wan" or "bleak." Linguist Saeki Umetomo's work *Kokugogaku taikei* (Outline of Japanese Linguistics) notes this semantic drift, where 蒼 could evoke not just hue but also a desolate mood, and Chūya here exploits this dual denotation. The title is his most explicit tribute to Verlaine's *Songs Without Words* collection. Published in *Bungakukai.*

Moonlit Beach
c. 1936 / February 1937
Likely composed before Fumiya's death. Ōoka sees the beach as a setting for Chūya's pre-loss escape, possibly conjured from memories of the Yamaguchi coast. In another late attempt to broaden his popular

reach, the poet published this piece in *Shinjoen* (New Woman's Garden) (1937–1959), a newly established variety and culture magazine.

Spring Will Come Again

c. December 1936 / February 1937

Chūya's rawest elegy. In a diary entry of December 12, 1936, under the title "Fumiya's Life," he wrote the same content about a family trip to Ueno Zoo, but it is unclear which was written first. Published with "Moonlight I & II" in *Bungakukai* as "Three Poems"—the only ones that openly point to Fumiya's death.

Moonlight – I & II

c. 1936 / February 1937

Probably based on Verlaine's "Mandoline," ("Mandolin") which features Tircis, Aminte, and other pastoral characters. In Verlaine's poem—which Claude Debussy scored as a choral piece—the mood is one of romantic joy, with multiple references to music and song.

The Village Clock

October 1933 / March 1937

Inspired by Haruo Satō's "My Grandfather Clock," this poem first appeared in *Shiki* as the second part of a long, six-section poem entitled "One Night's Fantasy." Chūya respected Satō's literary opinions and frequently mentioned him in his diary. One reason is that Satō had been a kind of tutor to Shinkichi Takahashi, whose *Dadaisuto Shinkichi no shi* (Poems of the Dadaist Shinkichi) was Chūya's first aesthetic guidebook.

Portrait of a Certain Man

October 1933 / March 1937

This poem first appeared in *Shiki* as the fourth, fifth and sixth sections of "One Night's Fantasy." Chūya cut sections 1 and 3—"Her" and "Her Room"—and also made them independent works; they are the source of the mysterious "she" in the final stanza. The "green oil" is anthracene oil. Derived from coal tar, it was used as a hair tonic and ingredient in various cosmetics of the day.

Chōmon Gorge in Winter
December 1936 / April 1937
The 12km-long gorge was named by geologist and painter Hokkai Takashima and runs between Hagi and Yamaguchi City. Designated a national scenic spot in 1923, it is famous for its unusual rock formations and seasonal changes in scenery. A monument to this poem stands at the gorge's Senshin Bridge. Published in *Bungakukai.*

Yoneko
c. October 1936 / December 1936
Published in *Pen*, a magazine launched by Mikasa Shobō Co. Ltd., which was founded in 1933 by translator Michinosuke Takeuchi. It is unclear when and where they met, but Chūya's French fluency made him a fit for Takeuchi's Francophile circle, while *Pen*, as a venue for literature in translation, provided Chūya with a niche stage.

Noon
c. 1937 / October 1937
Published in *Bungakukai*, this sharp-witted poem was penned as Chūya's health crashed in the summer of 1937 and was the last to see print before he died. It has been a textbook and anthology staple ever since the war. A Japanese proverb quips, "Cherry blossoms are dull without alcohol," and here Chūya seems to apply it to humanity: however attractive the people are, they lack spark. Ōoka called this piece his final jab at shallow beauty.

Kasuga Rhapsody
c. March 1937 / May 1937
Chūya's stay at Nakamura Kokyō Sanatorium in Chiba was dually

precipitated by grief over Fumiya's death and the years of heavy drinking that had ravaged his body and mind. Following two months of delirium and suicidal depression, he emerged in March, frail but defiant, and with a final burst of manic energy poured his grief into this chaotic masterpiece. Hideo Kobayashi, in his 1938 eulogy, marveled at its "wild, unrestrained cry," calling it a testament to Chūya's refusal to fade quietly into death. Published in *Bungakukai.*

Frog Voice
May 1937 / July 1937
The poet's last gasp was this visceral bow to nature, a motif rare in his late urban phase. Ōoka hears the frogs' croaking as an echo of vitality. Evoking the rural stillness of the Yamaguchi rice paddies that pulsed with the sound during Chūya's youth, the poem offers a stark contrast to its companion piece, "Voice of Life," which closes *Goat Songs* with an abstract meditation on human weakness. Published in *Bungakukai*, it stunned Chūya's peers with its primal energy.

Postscript
July 1937 / December 1938
Although the text did not survive, Chūya's original Postscript was by all accounts candid and terse. For the book's December release, his editors, led by Kobayashi, smoothed its rough paragraphs into something more wistful. Perhaps overly reverent in their concern for his legacy, they tempered the wording with a sheen of decorum that, as Tanaka believes, was incommensurate with Chūya's intent.

Photo Credits

All photos courtesy of the Nakahara Chūya Memorial Museum, with the following exceptions: Kenji Miyazawa, from *Kenji Miyazawa and Natural Stones* by Yukio Kitade, Seikyūsha, 2010; Tarō Tominaga, from *Tarō Tominaga* by Satoru Higuchi, Sunagoya Shobō, 1986; Yoshihiro Yasuhara, from *Nakahara Chūya's Letters – Friendship with Yoshihiro Yasuhara: Special Exhibition*, edited by the Chūya Nakahara Memorial Museum, 2012; Shinkichi Takahashi, from *The Complete Works of Shinkichi Takahashi, Vol. 2* by Shinkichi Takahashi, Seidosha, 1982; Tetsutarō Kawakami, *Collected Works of Great Intellect, Vol. 10 – Tetsutarō Kawakami*, Nihon Shobō, 1958; Shōhei Ōoka, from *Shinchō Japanese Literature Album, No. 67 – Shōhei Ōoka*, Shinchōsha, 1995; Hideo Kobayashi, from *Shinchō Japanese Literature Album, No. 30 – Chūya Nakahara*, Shinchōsha, 1985; memorial dedication, from *Nakahara Chūya Photo Collection* edited by Shin Uchida, Yamaguchi City Tourism Association, 1993.

To Access Audio Recordings for the Poems:

1. Check to be sure you have an Internet connection.
2. Type the URL below into your web browser.

https://www.tuttlepublishing.com/poetry-of-chuya-nakahara

For support, you can email us at info@tuttlepublishing.com.

"Books to Span the East and West"

Tuttle Publishing was founded in 1832 in the small New England town of Rutland, Vermont [USA]. Our core values remain as strong today as they were then—to publish best-in-class books which bring people together one page at a time. In 1948, we established a publishing outpost in Japan—and Tuttle is now a leader in publishing English-language books about the arts, languages and cultures of Asia. The world has become a much smaller place today and Asia's economic and cultural influence has grown. Yet the need for meaningful dialogue and information about this diverse region has never been greater. Over the past seven decades, Tuttle has published thousands of books on subjects ranging from martial arts and paper crafts to language learning and literature—and our talented authors, illustrators, designers and photographers have won many prestigious awards. We welcome you to explore the wealth of information available on Asia at **www.tuttlepublishing.com**.

First published by Tuttle Publishing, an imprint of Periplus Editions (HK) Ltd.

www.tuttlepublishing.com

LCCN Data in progress

ISBN: 978-4-8053-1897-3

29 28 27 26 5 4 3 2 1 2511UM
Printed in Malaysia

GPSR Representative
Matt Parsons, matt.parsons@upi2mbooks.hr
UPI-2M PLUS d.o.o., Medulićeva 20, 10000 Zagreb, Croatia

Distributed by:

North America, Latin America & Europe
Tuttle Publishing
364 Innovation Drive
North Clarendon
VT 05759 9436, USA
Tel: 1(802) 773 8930
Fax: 1(802) 773 6993
info@tuttlepublishing.com
www.tuttlepublishing.com

Asia Pacific
Berkeley Books Pte Ltd
3 Kallang Sector #04-01
Singapore 349278
Tel: (65) 6741 2178
Fax: (65) 6741 2179
inquiries@periplus.com.sg
www.tuttlepublishing.com

Japan
Tuttle Publishing
Yaekari Building, 3rd Floor
5-4-12 Osaki Shinagawa-ku
Tokyo 141 0032 Japan
Tel: 81 (3) 5437 0171
Fax: 81 (3) 5437 0755
sales@tuttle.co.jp
www.tuttle.co.jp